7 Steps From Burnout to Happiness

A Modern Approach to a Stress-Free Work Life with Renewed Productivity and Clarity on What Matters Most

Karren Romero

© **Copyright 2022 - All rights reserved.**

The content contained within this book may not be reproduced, duplicated or transmitted without direct written permission from the author or the publisher.

Under no circumstances will any blame or legal responsibility be held against the publisher, or author, for any damages, reparation, or monetary loss due to the information contained within this book, either directly or indirectly.

Legal Notice:

This book is copyright protected. It is only for personal use. You cannot amend, distribute, sell, use, quote or paraphrase any part, or the content within this book, without the consent of the author or publisher.

Disclaimer Notice:

Please note the information contained within this document is for educational and entertainment purposes only. All effort has been executed to present accurate, up to date, reliable, complete information. No warranties of any kind are declared or implied. Readers acknowledge that the author is not engaged in the rendering of legal, financial, medical or professional advice. The content within this book has been derived from various sources. Please consult a licensed professional before attempting any techniques outlined in this book.

By reading this document, the reader agrees that under no circumstances is the author responsible for any losses, direct or indirect, that are incurred as a result of the use of the information contained within this document, including, but not limited to, errors, omissions, or inaccuracies.

As a special thank you for purchasing this book, we would like to give you the e-book below:

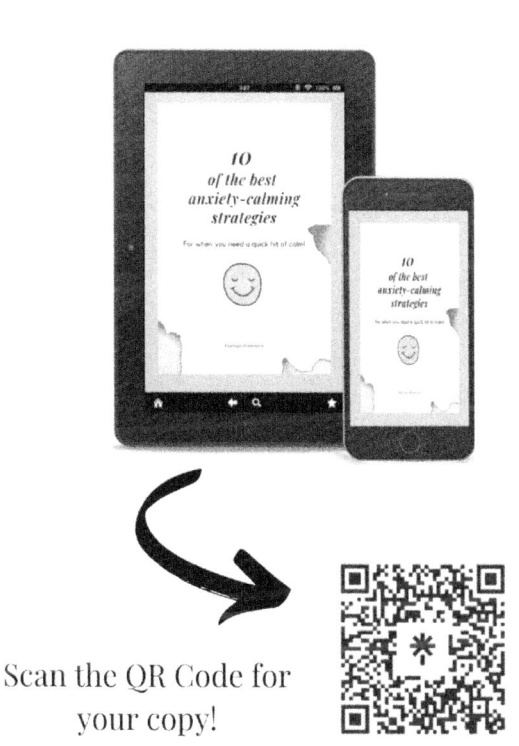

Scan the QR Code for your copy!

Table of Contents

INTRODUCTION 1
   BURNOUT: A GROWING PROBLEM? 3
      Why You Need This Book 4

CHAPTER 1: THE STRESS RESPONSE CYCLE 7
   BURNOUT AND THE STATE OF THE WORLD 7
      What Is Burnout? 8
      Reasons for Burnout 10
      Types of Burnout 14
      The Difference Between Burnout, Stress, Fatigue, and Exhaustion 15
   HOW STRESS AFFECTS YOUR BODY 17
      Central Nervous and Endocrine Systems 17
      Respiratory and Cardiovascular Systems 18
      Digestive System 18
      Muscular System 19
      Reproductive System 19
      Immune System 20
   HOW TO BREAK YOUR STRESS CYCLE 20
      How To Complete the Stress Cycle 21
   INTERACTIVE ELEMENT: BURNOUT SELF-TEST 24
      Interpretation of Results 30
   KEY TAKEAWAYS 32

CHAPTER 2: MOVE YOUR BODY 37
   THE BENEFITS OF EXERCISE 38
      Getting Started With Exercise 38
   SIMPLE EXERCISES TO GET YOU MOVING 39
      Tips For Making Your Workouts Successful 40
   HOW TO HAVE FUN WHILE EXERCISING 41
      Small Movements 42
      Have Fun While You Exercise 42
   KEY TAKEAWAYS 46

CHAPTER 3: IMAGINE TO WIN 49

WHY IS IMAGINATION IMPORTANT AND HOW SHOULD YOU USE YOURS? 49
   What Is Imagination? *50*
   Using Your Imagination *52*
  USING THE POWER OF YOUR IMAGINATION TO OVERCOME STRESS 53
   Guided Imagery *53*
  INTERACTIVE ELEMENT: VISUAL IMAGERY 55
  KEY TAKEAWAYS 57

CHAPTER 4: EXPRESS YOURSELF 61

  CREATIVE SELF-EXPRESSION 62
   The Benefits of Self-Expression *63*
  TYPES OF CREATIVE EXPRESSION 64
   Mindful Creativity Can Teach Us Self-Expression *65*
  EXPRESSING YOURSELF THROUGH HUMOR 66
  THE BENEFITS OF CRYING 67
  INTERACTIVE ELEMENT: CREATIVE JOURNALING 68
   Creative Journaling Ideas *69*
  KEY TAKEAWAYS 72

CHAPTER 5: REST & SLEEP 76

  WHY YOU NEED SLEEP 77
   Your Internal Body Clock *77*
   Good Reasons To Get More Sleep *80*
   Why The Quality of Your Sleep Is Important *81*
  SLEEP CHRONOTYPES 83
   What Determines Your Chronotype? *84*
  INTERACTIVE ELEMENT: CHRONOTYPE QUIZ 86
  KEY TAKEAWAYS 89

CHAPTER 6: MINDFUL PAUSE 92

  THE POWER OF PAUSE 92
   Two Types of Noise *93*
   Ways of Pausing *94*
  INTERACTIVE ELEMENT: GUIDED MEDITATION AND DEEP BREATHING EXERCISES . 95
   How To Do Guided Meditation *95*
   How To Practice Deep Breathing *96*
  KEY TAKEAWAYS 99

CHAPTER 7: SELF-COMPASSION 102

  WHAT IS SELF-COMPASSION? 102
   Practicing Self-Compassion *103*

Techniques for Improving Your Self-Compassion 105
REDUCING SELF-CRITICISM 107
Challenging Your Negative Self-Talk 109
Examples of Negative Self-Talk 110
Changing Your Negative Self-Talk 111
Positive Affirmations 113
INTERACTIVE ELEMENT: SELF-COMPASSION JOURNAL 115
Writing Prompts for Your Self-Compassion Journal 118
KEY TAKEAWAYS 120

CHAPTER 8: BUILD CONNECTIONS 125

WHY DO WE NEED TO CONNECT? 125
Random Acts of Kindness 127
The Stress-Reducing Conversations 129
The Importance of Physical Connection 131
Spirituality 135
Why You Should Sometimes Put Yourself First 138
INTERACTIVE ELEMENT: SELF-CARE LIST 140
KEY TAKEAWAYS 141

CONCLUSION 146

A CONSTANT STATE OF STRESS: COMPLETING YOUR STRESS CYCLE 147
IMAGINATION AND CREATIVITY CAN GIVE YOU A BETTER LIFE 148
EXPRESSING YOUR EMOTIONS 149
THE PHYSICAL ASPECTS OF BURNOUT 150
TAKING A BREAK AND PAUSING 150
TAKING CARE OF YOURSELF 151

PERSONAL NOTE FROM THE AUTHOR 152

REFERENCES 154

Introduction

Burnout is what happens when you try to avoid being human for too long.

—Michael Gungor

The year 2020 was supposed to be the year for me, but fate seemed to have other things planned. The year started with a bang, and it felt like our plans were finally falling into place, but then, things quickly went sour in spring with the outbreak of Covid-19.

As a nurse working on the front line, I witnessed the overwhelming surge of patients coming in for treatment. Like myself, many nurses from different specialties were called to help care for critically ill patients in the Intensive Care Unit (ICU). Luckily, I have reasonable experience in critical care nursing and so I was eager to assist. That same day, I put on a hazmat suit, an FFP3 mask, and off I went.

The hospital corridors which were once loud and busy now looked empty and desolate. It's as if an apocalypse just happened. I was quickly distracted by the large signs outside of every ward I walked past that read "STOP! You are entering a Covid-19 isolation area. Restricted access only." The hospital was unrecognizable.

The first shift was brutal. Within a few hours, the once quiet and empty unit was full of nurses and doctors wearing personal protective equipment. Everyone was scrambling to intubate patients, insert intravenous lines and administer medication in an attempt to save patients' lives. While this was all happening, there was an odd silence between us all. It's as if there was an unspoken feeling of fear and panic between us, but we kept working. Stay focused, keep going, I would say to myself, as I gave CPR to my patient. This was the moment I realized we would now be the front-line Covid-19 nurses.

The sheer influx of patients quickly overwhelmed the hospital and so more and more wards had to be closed and were quickly converted into makeshift critical care units. More nurses from different specialties were also redeployed to these units to help with the surge, but it just felt like a losing battle. Despite my best efforts, my patients were still dying. I started to doubt myself and I was starting to feel like I wasn't good enough. A few weeks in, the adrenaline rush started to fade. This was replaced by anxiety, fear, and exhaustion. We battled Covid-19 in plastic hazmat suits with sweat running down our bodies, and masks that would rub our skin raw to protect ourselves. We couldn't risk taking Covid home with us, especially those of us who had family members who were at high risk of becoming sick or dying from the virus.

As the months passed, we learned more about the virus, and the search for the vaccine treatment intensified, as well as the testing. Summer would come and everything was going to go back to how it was before, I thought to myself. When I came home at night, parking my bike outside my home, my neighborhood cheered us on with their pots and pans outside. This gave me brief moments of joy and hope that it was going to get better. Still, I was exhausted. I would cry as soon as I left work and felt anxious and nervous every time I left the house. I thought about skipping work, but I also thought about my colleagues who were there day in and day out. I thought about my patients, and I couldn't let them down. So, I kept going. At this point, the sleepless nights and nightmares were getting worse. I stopped showing up for any social activities and ignored phone calls from my family and friends. My bubbly and outgoing personality was losing its spark and was slowly fading away. I became cynical and struggled to show compassion. I was at breaking point, but I didn't recognize the signs and continued to think that I was doing fine. Sure, it was just stress! So, I convinced myself that all I needed was some time off. Still, a few days of rest did not help and did little to stop my thoughts from becoming even darker and more negative. At this point, I realized that things would have to change soon.

My hope is that sharing the insights that I've gained on my journey back from burnout, will prevent you from falling into the same dark hole. If you're already in that hole, I hope it helps you find your way out.

Let's start by taking a look at how others are experiencing burnout.

Burnout: A Growing Problem?

The fact is, stress is a major part of the world of work. There will always be a difficult manager with unreasonable expectations who doesn't see you as a shining star. Gossipy, backstabbing colleagues might not make your time at the office any easier. Put long hours into the mix and it could have serious consequences for your health and well-being.

Burnout is a worldwide problem that's not going away any time soon. While Covid normalized remote work which saves us travel time, some are becoming victims of burnout because of the long hours worked at home. If you're an extrovert who gets

3

your energy from socializing, this could also impact your mental health negatively.

Deloitte conducted a recent survey with over 1,000 respondents, where over 77% of people working from the office said they've experienced burnout in their jobs (Apollo Technical, 2022). 91% of the participants said that stress impacts the quality of their work, while 83% said burnout negatively affected their personal relationships.

Many people also feel their employers aren't doing enough to help people prevent burnout, or to help employees recover from it.

A survey by Owl Labs found that 92% of the people they reached out to expected to work from home one or more days per week; 80% expected to work from home for more than three days a week (Apollo Technical, 2022).

While many people feel they're more productive when working from home, others just feel trapped. The risk of burnout is also high if you're a remote worker. It seems people who have started doing remote work for the first time during the pandemic are struggling to separate their home from work lives.

Burnout is very real, and it is happening both in the office and remote work settings.

Why You Need This Book

Reading this book can help you understand burnout and answer these questions:

Why are you burned out?

How can you use creative self-expression to recover from burnout?

Why do you need to exercise regularly and sleep well?

How can connecting to others improve your health?

Why should you practice mindfulness?

This book will help give you the confidence that you can make the necessary changes to your life. You need to act when you recognize the warning signs, as it can be a long journey back from burnout. You are empowered with the practical tools to prevent burnout and practice self-care.

You are valuable, and you need to accept that you're allowed to care for yourself. Be proud that you've started the journey to become a healthier version of yourself and be confident that you can travel this journey to the end. I am excited in completing this journey with you!

Chapter 1:

The Stress Response Cycle

Your stress level has probably increased a lot over the last few years. Most of us have been affected by the Covid-19 pandemic that overwhelmed the globe in 2020. You may have lost loved ones or friends to Covid, and even if you didn't, you're likely suffering as a result of the socio-economic challenges caused by the pandemic and other geopolitical problems.

We're working harder than ever before just to make ends meet. Some of us even take on side hustles on top of our full-time jobs and do these after-hours to survive until the end of the month. Worldwide, people are in financial trouble and it's forecasted that most leading economies will fall into recession during 2023. On social media, people admit to working 70-hour weeks to be able to pay their bills and passing by their marriage partners and children like ships on their way to different ports. One can just imagine the devastating consequences to your physical and mental health, not to mention families breaking apart if this situation should continue for an extended period.

Burnout and the State of the World

The pandemic has also changed how we work, with many people permanently switching to remote work, blurring the line between our home and work lives. Our stress levels would have increased even more as a result of this situation. In many cases, switching off from work became increasingly complex, and some companies now expect their staff to be available 24/7. Many of us even find ourselves working on weekends, while for some, sick days have become a thing of the past.

As the world slowly returns to a state we can regard as more "normal," we need to be aware that stress and anxiety will not just disappear, especially with all the other ongoing problems we're still facing. It's even predicted that Covid-19 can make a comeback and that we should be prepared to face more waves in the future.

We shouldn't let our guard down when it comes to our mental health. Surging stress levels and burnout can only lengthen the recovery phase if we don't prioritize our mental health and well-being.

We're always told we need to learn time management to control our stress levels, but you may actually need to focus more on managing your energy levels than your time, especially when it comes to burnout. Your energy levels will determine what you achieve at the end of the day. Getting anything done is difficult when you're burned out and exhausted. Your productivity will decrease, and you'll become less effective in all areas of your life.

What Is Burnout?

While burnout can creep up on you, you'll recognize the symptoms when they hit you full-on. You can try to keep going by drinking excessive amounts of coffee and energy drinks or eating sugary and fatty foods. However, soon you'll be emotionally, physically, and mentally exhausted. This can happen if you have been exposed to excessive stress for an extended period. You might be feeling overwhelmed and like you can no longer deal with the constant demands in your personal and professional life.

For many people, the trip down the slippery slope to burnout starts when they have unmeetable goals and demands. They get to a stage where their brains can't handle it any longer, and something has to give.

They become more and more frustrated until they give into despair. They get trapped in a cycle between hating their jobs and feeling they can't leave as they need the money to raise their children and pay their bills.

Long-term burnout is also worrying because it can cause changes to your body and make you more vulnerable to illness. Therefore, it's best to deal with burnout as soon as possible when you recognize the symptoms.

If you pay attention to the early symptoms, you can prevent a major breakdown.

Symptoms

Burnout has some painful and tiring physical symptoms, like exhaustion—you have to drag yourself out of bed every morning and barely make it there. On days like these, you're glad you're using public transport, as you won't even be able to pay attention to driving a car. Your mind only wakes up after several cups of coffee.

You could also be ill all the time. You pick up every single illness the kids bring from school, making you even more stressed as you become increasingly unpopular for taking so many sick days.

Burnout can also cause you to sleep poorly and wake up several times a night. Sometimes you may struggle to fall asleep. You're eating more than ever and relying on sugar and coffee to get you through the long days, which leads to weight gain.

You have frequent headaches and muscle pain, which makes it even more of a drag to get through the day.

The emotional fallout of burnout can also get you down. Self-doubt can make you feel like a failure when things start to go wrong at work. The reactions of coworkers often don't help, especially when people start playing the blame game, and no one wants to take personal responsibility. Before you become too pessimistic and cynical and take your frustrations out on them, remember that your colleagues could also have lost their motivation for their jobs as a result of burnout. Burned out employees often lose their feelings of accomplishment, which decreases their satisfaction in the workplace.

If you're an extrovert, one of the symptoms can also be that you start to isolate yourself more and more from other people. You might also find yourself procrastinating at work and home and taking forever to get things done.

Reasons for Burnout

There are several reasons and types of burnout, and you need to know something about these to protect yourself from burning out or recover from it.

The reasons for burnout in the workplace are apparent, yet it continues to happen, and employees and their employers pay the price.

Some of the main reasons include unmanageable workloads and unfair treatment. In many workplaces, the high performers and hard workers often end up with the bulk of the work and responsibilities. People can become ill from stress, but they're still expected to carry most of the load, while inefficient employees sometimes get to cruise along without severe consequences. This is not always the case, but it's easier for unmotivated employees to hide in departments where it is expected that one or two efficient employees have to carry others.

This type of unfair treatment can induce or worsen burnout. If you're a high performer, you're often expected to keep up this pace, and if you make one unfortunate error, it can be held against you. However, your underperforming coworkers continue making mistakes without raising eyebrows.

If you find yourself working in a place like this, remember that it's never worth sacrificing your health to satisfy the unreasonable demands of someone else, such as your managers at work. When your health is affected, getting it back to the state it was before might be tough, especially if you have to continue working in this environment. Ultimately, it's not reasonable to sacrifice your health to put big money into someone else's pocket. If your work environment is toxic, your best option could be to find a way out as soon as possible. Or you could opt out of your exploitative work culture by quite quitting.

Quiet Quitting

This term has gone into circulation fairly recently and describes a new way of dealing with workplace burnout.

When you "quiet quit," as it's called in the popular dialogue, you're not actually quitting your job, but you're doing only the basics instead of walking the so-called extra mile. Basically, you only do enough to keep your job. This term only seems to have been around since August last year, which just shows you what a serious issue burnout has become.

While some people regard it as a negative concept that could cost you your job or be bad for your long-term career, others see it as perfectly acceptable and would suggest people have been doing this for years. You may have had coworkers who refuse to do more than what is indicated in their job description.

Those of us who are slightly older and have had a toxic work ethic (you have to work hard even if you have to sacrifice your own health) drilled into us may struggle with the concept of quiet quitting. However, it's popular among younger generations who refuse to bow down to toxic workplace cultures.

Think or say about it what you want, but quiet quitting could prevent burnout or help you recover from burnout. Burnout is often the result of cultural expectations rather than actual work requirements. For example, some employers could expect their employees to be available and obedient at all times. You throw off these expectations if you're a quiet quitter.

Quiet quitting is a helpful strategy if you feel trapped in your job.

It's a good strategy when you can't escape your stressor. It doesn't necessarily mean not doing your job, but it can simply mean changing your approach to your work and that you don't have to burn yourself out for the sake of work. For example, you can go from taking on large amounts of extra work and working at all hours to just sticking to your regular hours. Remember, tomorrow is another day. Quiet quitting could also involve growing thick skin. The idea is that it enables you to ignore managers and coworkers who place unnecessary pressure on you, e.g., those who want to get the job done at any cost, often because they're often not involved in having to do it themselves.

When Is Quiet Quitting For You?

Quiet quitting might be for you if you're the type of person who has put a great deal of effort into their work, and much of your self-worth is also derived from the kind of job you do. For example, your self-esteem gets a boost when you're promoted to a management position.

In this case, it will be better for your mental health to detach your self-worth from your unreasonable working conditions. You're so much more valuable than any contribution you make at work.

At first, you might feel a sense of loss and even sadness. However, soon you'll find meaning in new activities once you're able to get the idea out of your head that you should commit your whole being to your job.

Confusing or changing work responsibilities can also add fuel to the burnout fire. Just when you have the handle on one task, the process changes, or more tasks get dumped on you. Employees are then held accountable for becoming confused with this way of working and not keeping up with the multiple changes. If your workplace functions this way, it's probably best to protect yourself against burnout by growing thick skin.

If you're burned out, you've likely experienced a lack of support and proper communication from your managers. This can go hand-in-hand with confusing work responsibilities. Just when you think you're on the right path, you get pushed off in another direction. If you have a manager who's just interested in performing and squeezing the last bit of work out of you to achieve something, don't expect them to understand when you're experiencing a health or family crisis.

Hectic deadline pressure can also push you over the deadline edge. It's important to push back against this, as your health will always be more important. Remember that while you're replaceable at work, your family and loved ones can't replace you.

Types of Burnout

There are actually three types of burnout with different causes:

- **Overload burnout** usually happens when you're beyond driven in your pursuit of success. You don't mind risking your health and personal life to be successful at your job.

- **Under-challenged burnout** happens when you're bored at your job, and you could distance yourself from it and avoid responsibilities. It's possible there are no growth opportunities or opportunities for learning and training. Beware of companies that don't invest in their employees.

- **Neglect burnout** is probably the saddest kind. You feel helpless and incapable of keeping up with your responsibilities. This can also be connected to imposter syndrome, where you would doubt your talents, skills, or accomplishments.

The Difference Between Burnout, Stress, Fatigue, and Exhaustion

Interestingly, burnout was initially regarded as a syndrome that resulted from workplace stress not being managed successfully. Its three main symptoms were said to be feelings of exhaustion, an increased mental distance from your job, and feeling increasingly negative toward your job, which led to you becoming less efficient. It was said that burnout shouldn't be used to describe experiences in other life areas.

Many companies are taking burnout more seriously now that it's regarded as a workplace crisis. It's vital to understand that burnout isn't the same as stress, and you can't fix it by working fewer hours, taking a long holiday, or slowing down in general. When you're under stress, you still struggle to cope with pressure. Once you're burned out, you've given up all hope of overcoming your obstacles. You start to believe that all your efforts are useless and that you'll be wasting your time no matter what you do. You can't even meet the smallest obligations and even doing a small task feels like climbing a huge mountain.

It might also be that you're fatigued. You could be feeling weak and tired, and many people think that fatigue and tiredness are the same thing. However, there's a significant difference. Fatigue is constant and can last for years, but you can recover pretty quickly from being tired. Your fatigue could be physical, mental, or even due to a combination of factors.

As a result of our hectic modern lifestyle, we're all at risk of falling prey to some of these factors. You have a lifestyle of staying up late, drinking lots of alcohol and caffeine, and you like eating pizza every other night of the week. You're simply not a fan of healthy food. After all, you're not really living your life when you're eating leaves like a rabbit. Your body is too tired to force it to do exercise, and you walk only when you really have to.

Your job has become a nightmare of long shifts, 7-day work weeks, and not to mention boredom. Just the thought of going there is making you anxious and depressed. However, the situation can still be remedied if you learn some stress management techniques and work on improving your lifestyle.

Exhaustion is a shorter-lived type of fatigue that can also get you down emotionally, physically, and mentally. However, if periods of exhaustion build up, you can become fatigued and then burned out.

So how do you really tell the difference between exhaustion, fatigue, and burnout? The easiest way is to see how long it takes you to recover.

If all it takes is a good night's sleep, a nutritious meal, and a relaxing shower, then you're likely suffering from tiredness.

If you can get going again after a two-week holiday focused on de-stressing and unplugging, you suffer from exhaustion. However, it might take you a couple of months to overcome fatigue.

If you're burned out, the situation might take longer to fix. It will depend on your overall condition and also how long you've been burned out. It could help a lot if you can learn some coping strategies for burnout, like practicing meditation.

An excellent way to manage all these conditions is to tune into your own needs. Look at your work-life balance and practice some healthy ways to unwind. It's also essential to make sure you get enough sleep.

Be in touch with your emotions and try to manage them to the best of your ability. Emotional or psychological strain can cause you to act erratically even if you're not physically tired. Keep in touch with your loved ones and create a healthy support network.

How Stress Affects Your Body

Most of us know stress is bad for your mental health, but it can also be bad for the rest of your body, from your nervous to your reproductive system.

Central Nervous and Endocrine Systems

You've probably heard of your fight-or-flight response. Well, stress can trigger this response, which is controlled by your central nervous system (CNS).

When you feel stressed, your brain sends signals through your body. The stress hormones in your body will increase, and you'll feel this as your heart will beat faster.

Your nervous system will return to normal once the stress has passed, but if you have chronic stress, your body will stay in a defensive response. This can send you looking for ways to get rid of the bad feelings. It can be challenging to stay away from alcohol or drugs or reach for comfort foods that are mostly unhealthy. Or you may just not feel like eating at all.

Respiratory and Cardiovascular Systems

When you're stressed, you may find breathing more difficult, especially if you suffer from a condition like asthma, chronic bronchitis, or emphysema.

The extra adrenaline in your body will also increase blood flow, while your heart rate and blood pressure will increase as your body pumps more blood to your heart, other vital organs, and muscles to get them ready for action.

If you're constantly stressed for a long time, your heart will have to work harder, which could push your blood pressure up and could even cause you to have a heart attack or stroke.

Digestive System

If you constantly have stomach pain, bloating, nausea, constipation, and diarrhea, it could be because of stress. It could also trigger irritable bowel syndrome (IBS) and worsen it.

Stress could also cause you to develop type 2 diabetes or worsen if you already suffer from it.

Muscular System

We've all had this painful experience. You're already stressed, rolling around at night because you can't sleep, and your muscles tense up. Painful neck, shoulder, and back pain is often a result of stress. Have you been sitting in one position at work too long because you need to meet hectic deadlines? That could explain your lower back pain.

The muscles will usually relax once the stress passes, but you may experience pain for longer periods of time if you have chronic stress.

Reproductive System

Stress can make you mentally and physically tired, and you may find yourself avoiding sex. In women who suffer from premenstrual syndrome or PMS, your symptoms could also worsen, and your periods could get heavier and more painful. They could even become irregular. When you're having a stressful month, you'll usually find that your period and PMS are worse than during times you aren't stressed.

If you're going through menopause, your symptoms will also be worse during a stressful time because of an increase in hormone levels.

You could also struggle to get pregnant, and stress can complicate pregnancy.

Chronic stress can cause men's testosterone levels to drop, impact their sperm levels and lead to issues like impotence, erectile dysfunction, or infections in the prostate or testes.

Immune System

Chronic stress will weaken your immune system, and you'll find it takes you longer to recover after you get sick or become injured. You'll also catch viruses easier, such as colds, flu, and Covid-19.

How to Break Your Stress Cycle

These days, it's not uncommon to feel like we're in a constant state of stress. Stressors are all around us, and many of us never complete our stress cycles. A stress cycle can have many phases, and we complete one when our bodies learn we're safe after facing danger.

The danger is that if we don't confront our stress, our bodies will stay in a constant state of activation with increased blood pressure, putting us at a higher chance of developing heart disease and digestion issues. Therefore, completing a stress cycle is very important for our health.

When it comes to the stress cycle, it's important to know that there are different stages:

1. Stage one is when the external stressor or triggering event happens. For example, someone says something to you that makes you unhappy.

2. At stage two, your senses start to realize something has gone wrong and send information to your amygdala (this is the part of your brain that processes information like fear and anger). When your amygdala is activated, a

signal goes to your hypothalamus and pituitary gland, which are responsible for keeping the balance in your body.

3. When you reach stage three, your sympathetic nervous system is activated, and your body goes into fight or flight response mode. It's then that your heart rate starts going up, and your immune and digestive systems are negatively affected.

4. At stage four, you'll start to notice the stress. Your symptoms, such as increased heart rate and body aches, will now become more noticeable than at stage 3. You may now start worrying about how well you're handling stress and feel worried and anxious.

5. Stage five, the final stage of the cycle, has to do with how you cope with your stress. You're starting to look for ways to deal with your discomfort. However, if you manage it in a maladaptive way, you might actually increase your stress. These strategies could work in the short term, but you'll end up with much worse problems in the long term. These strategies, which are also toxic to your mental health, can include using drugs and/or alcohol, constantly checking your cell phone, or overworking. If you use these strategies, you could find yourself in a hyper-aroused state and more stressed out than before.

How To Complete the Stress Cycle

Getting at least two hours of physical activity a week is important. This can include walking, swimming, dancing, or anything that you enjoy doing that gets you moving.

Creativity can also help you complete the cycle. Do something you enjoy, whether it is writing, gardening, or cooking. Laughing is an easy way to release bottled-up emotions. Watch a funny movie or visit some friends who always make you laugh.

You can also release stress through deep breathing exercises such as yoga and tai chi.

One of the most important things is ensuring you get enough rest, as a good night's sleep can help your body recover from stressful events.

Physical affection and touch from a loved one can make you feel safe. Crying is another way your body can release stress, and you should never try repressing your tears.

The Difference Between Stress and Stressors

You need to understand the difference between stress and stressors to be able to complete the stress response cycle and recover from burnout.

Stress

Stress releases hormones in your body, namely cortisol and adrenaline, which put your body into fight or flight mode. This is when you struggle to make decisions, and your immune system and digestion are already affected. If you were part of early mankind, it means you probably would have been able to escape a predator, but in our modern world, it only cripples your decision-making ability. And as said before, if this carries on for a long time, your health will take a knock.

Stressors

Most people will see stress as something in their lives outside of themselves that they can't control. For most people, this would be work and money. So, the things that cause stress are "stressors," while "stress" is your reaction to these stressors.

Stress will always be there, and a lot of the time, you won't be able to avoid your stressors. But you *can* manage your reaction to them. This can include healthy coping mechanisms like meditation.

Interactive Element: Burnout Self-Test

The self-assessment explores the risk of burnout by looking at exhaustion, depersonalization, and personal achievement. The tool can give you some helpful insight, but you shouldn't use it as a clinical diagnostic technique. At every question, indicate the score that corresponds to your response. Add up your scores for the sections and then compare your results with the interpretation at the bottom of the assessment.

Questions	Never	A Few Times a Year	Once a Months	A Few Times per Month	Once a Week	A Few Times per Week	Every Day
Section A	0	1	2	3	4	5	6
My job drains me emotionally.							
I need to make a lot of effort when I work with people.							

My job frustrates me.								
I feel my work is destroying my spirit.								
I feel I work too hard.								
I feel I'm at the end of my tether.								
It stresses me too much to work with people.								
Score – SECTION A								

Section B	0	1	2	3	4	5	6
I deal with my coworkers in an impersonal way, almost as if they're objects.							
I'm already tired when I get up in the morning and have to go to work.							
It seems to me that my colleagues are holding me responsible for some of their problems.							
I don't care about what happens to my colleagues or team.							

I don't have patience after a day at work.								
I have become insensitive toward people in the workplace.								
It feels as if this job is making me uncaring.								
Score – SECTION B								
Section C	0	1	2	3	4	5	6
I feel that I accomplish worthwhile things in my job.								
I am energetic.								

It's easy for me to understand what my coworkers feel.							
I can look after my coworker's problems effectively.							
I am able to handle problems at work very calmly.							
I feel that I have a positive influence on people.							

I can create a relaxed atmosphere with my coworkers.							
I am refreshed after I have spent time with my coworkers.							
Total score – SECTION C							

Interpretation of Results

Compare your results to the list below.

Section A - Burnout

You can measure your level of burnout according to the following results:

30 and over: High-level burnout

Between 18 and 29: Moderate burnout

17 or less: Low-level burnout

Section B: Depersonalization (Loss of empathy)

12 and higher: High-level burnout

Between 6 and 11: Moderate burnout

5 or less: low-level burnout

Section C: Personal Achievement (Are you demotivated and feel like you're not accomplishing anything?)

More than 40: Low-level burnout

Between 34 and 39: Moderate burnout

33 or less: High-level burnout

If you have achieved a high score in the first two sections and a low score in the last section, you may be experiencing burnout.

Remember that the test is not a clinical analysis. You still need to consult a doctor or mental health professional if you need help with stress management or if you think you may be dealing with burnout.

Key Takeaways

- Burnout could creep up on you, but you will recognize the symptoms when they fully hit you. Many become emotionally, mentally, and physically exhausted and then try to keep going by eating unhealthy food and drinking excessive amounts of coffee and energy drinks.

- Long-term burnout could also make you more vulnerable to illness. You can get sick more easily, but in the long term, you could also develop chronic conditions such as high blood pressure and heart problems.

- The symptoms of burnout can be painful and tiring and include exhaustion, frequent illness, and disrupted sleep.

- You can start feeling like a failure when things go wrong at work. You may end up not wanting to go to work at all. If you work in a toxic environment, "quiet quitting" might be an option if you're not able to leave your job.

- Burnout could also cause you to procrastinate at work and at home. You might feel like you just do not have the energy to get things done, and you could find yourself constantly distracted, e.g., by spending time on social media when your mind is unable to focus.

- Unmanageable workloads and unfair treatment are some of the main reasons for burnout in the workplace. The high performers and hard workers often end up with the bulk of their work and responsibilities in toxic work environments, especially where there is insufficient management capacity.

- Confusing or constantly changing work responsibilities can also add to burnout. For example, just when you are used to certain processes at work, they change, or more work gets dumped on you.

- In work environments with burnout, there is often a lack of support from managers and confusing work responsibilities.

- Hectic deadlines can also contribute to burnout.

- People who suffer from overload burnout are usually people who are very driven to achieve success. These people don't mind risking their health and personal lives to succeed at their jobs.

- Under-challenged burnout usually happens to people who are bored at their jobs and don't have opportunities for learning and training.

- People who suffer from imposter syndrome and doubt their talents and accomplishments can become victims of neglect burnout. This can make them feel helpless and as if they're unable to keep up with their responsibilities.

- It is essential to understand that burnout isn't the same as stress. You can't fix burnout by working fewer hours, slowing down, or taking a long holiday.

- You can manage your burnout, fatigue, and exhaustion by tuning into your own needs. Think carefully about your workplace balance and consider healthy ways to help you unwind. Make sure you get enough sleep.

- You could be feeling weak and tired, but it's important to realize that fatigue and tiredness aren't the same thing. The difference is that you could feel constantly fatigued, which could even last for years. When you're tired, you can generally recover quickly, even after a good night's sleep.

- It's not uncommon to feel constantly stressed, as stress is all around us, and we can find it in all aspects of our lives. Many people never complete their stress cycles, which is very important, as you need to complete your stress cycle for your body to feel safe and learn that it's no longer in danger.

- Completing a stress cycle is essential for your health. If we don't confront our stress, our bodies will stay in a constant state of activation, and we could develop all kinds of health issues, like high blood pressure, heart problems, and digestion issues.

- Exercise can help you a great deal when it comes to completing your stress cycle. Do anything you enjoy or that gets you moving, such as swimming, dancing, or jogging. Not everyone enjoys going to the gym, so exercising outside is perfectly acceptable, for example, if you want to go jogging.

- Creative activities can also help you complete your stress cycle. Do something enjoyable to you, such as writing, painting, baking a cake, or whatever activities you enjoy.

- Make sure you get enough sleep, as sleep is instrumental in helping you recover from stress, fatigue, tiredness, exhaustion, and burnout.

- Most people will see stress as something outside of themselves that they can't control, such as work and money. These stressors and your reaction to them are the stress you experience.

- Stress will always be a massive part of life, and you won't be able to avoid your stressors. That is why learning to manage your reaction to them is essential.

Chapter 2:

Move Your Body

I feel stressed as I put my yoga mat down after a long day at work. I struggle to organize my thoughts and feel as if I just want to get away from myself. Of course, that's not possible, but exercise is the next best thing for me.

The hot air in the room opens up my lungs as I breathe in and out, loosening up my tense muscles. My headache disappears almost immediately. As I complete each pose and become more aware of my breath, my mind becomes quiet. I feel my heart beating and slowing down as I breathe, creating stillness. My muscles feel strong and re-energized. Sweat drips down my body, and I feel gratitude for my mind, body, and breath.

When I finally open my eyes, I had forgotten that I was ever stressed. My mind is relaxed and happy. I'm at peace with the world.

The relaxing feeling you experience after a workout is a result of your body completing its stress cycle. You've managed to turn off your flight-or-fight response, and you're safe again.

The Benefits of Exercise

Exercise can have many benefits for your physical health. Many of us struggle to stick to exercise routines that we don't enjoy, so the trick is to find something you enjoy doing.

Getting Started With Exercise

It's never too late to start exercising, but you need to take it slow if you haven't done any exercise for a long time or speak to your doctor to ensure your health is good enough to start exercising.

Exercise has long-term benefits like reducing your risk of developing heart disease and diabetes and strengthening your bones and muscles. Still, once you really get into it, you'll also discover some useful short-term benefits.

It can help you control your weight. Now, don't rush out, buy a scale, and weigh yourself daily. This is not a healthy way of living. You'll find that you naturally lose some weight while doing exercise. Even if it's not a lot of weight, you'll end up being healthier, and you'll feel fitter.

If you're a smoker, exercise can also help you quit. It can help reduce cravings and withdrawal symptoms and limit your weight gain after quitting.

Exercise is also a fantastic mood booster. When you exercise, your body releases chemicals that will improve your mood and make you feel relaxed. The stress of the day will disappear, and you also face a lower risk of developing depression.

Simple Exercises To Get You Moving

When it comes to fitness, we all have to start at the beginning. Even super-fit people and professional athletes had to start from scratch long ago when they were all inexperienced children. If you haven't exercised in a long time, or you're only starting now, beginner workouts are an excellent way to introduce your body to exercise. If you have any health issues, you need to see your doctor for a physical and get their advice before you start exercising. Remember, you need to be safe when you exercise, as the aim is to benefit your health and not harm it.

Your best bet is to build a weekly workout program that focuses on different components of fitness, which will help you get in shape quickly and reduce your risk of injury. Focus on these five areas to make progress faster when it comes to your fitness and endurance: muscular strength, cardiovascular endurance, flexibility, muscular endurance, and body composition.

"Cardio" is the type of exercise that makes your heart beat faster. If you're a beginner, you could even start with something as simple as taking a fast walk every day. Or you could even walk for 5 to 10 minutes a few times a day. Short bits of exercise add up at the end of the day or week and can also improve your overall fitness and health.

Any form of cardio, such as running, swimming, cycling, rowing, or using exercise machines, is really good for you, as it elevates your heart rate and makes you breathe harder, which gets more oxygen into your body and circulates it to your muscles.

Cardio will help you improve your endurance, get your body to build more calories by increasing your metabolic rate, and will also help you build muscle mass.

If you're just starting out, you should focus on light to moderate exercise. For example, if you choose jogging, you can start by doing a bit of walking, running for a bit, and then alternating again. Make sure you walk for a few minutes and then jog for 30 to 60 seconds.

You could also walk for another one to two minutes before jogging for 30 to 60 seconds. You can aim to do about 10 to 20 minutes, depending on your current level of fitness. Remember that for the sake of your health and wellness, you can gradually increase your workout intensity. If you're a beginner, you shouldn't do cardio for more than 20 minutes.

You can build muscle strength and endurance in different ways. You can use resistance machines and different kinds of weights, equally, you could even use your own body weight. You don't have to go to the gym. You could work out at home or even outside your home. There's no healthier way to exercise than doing it outside in the fresh air. Strength training workouts with a higher number of reps with lower weights can help you increase your muscle endurance.

Tips For Making Your Workouts Successful

You can make sure that your exercise sessions are successful by doing the following:

- You need to be kind to your body if you want to make exercising a long-term habit. Before you start exercising, warm up by doing a few minutes of easy cardio exercise.

- Doing stretches before and after you work out can help you prevent soreness.

- Start with alternating rest and exercise days and do at least three workouts per week. You should slowly increase your workouts to four or five workouts per week.

- If your body feels tired or you feel pain, stop exercising immediately, or don't drag yourself to the gym or force yourself to go for a run. There's no point in exercising if you're going to do more damage than good.

- If you are in pain after working out, rest the next day, even if you plan to work out the next day.

How To Have Fun While Exercising

If you hate exercise, it's going to make it extra difficult for you to start and get into a routine. However, there are ways to enjoy exercise, get fit and even lose some weight in the process.

The trick is to exercise in a way that doesn't feel like exercise.

Maybe you don't have the time or strength to hit the gym. That's fine because the best exercise routine is the one you actually end up doing.

Here are some interesting ways to get some more exercise and movement in your life.

Small Movements

Small movements or fidgeting can help you burn more calories in a day. It's not good for us to sit all day long, so make sure you get on your feet, even if you pace around your office.

If you think about it, we're constantly looking for easier and faster ways to do things, striving to be as efficient as possible. But you could actually lose more weight if you are less efficient in other ways.

For example, stand up more frequently or park further away at work or the grocery store. Maybe you'll get slightly less work done, or your shopping will take more time, but each extra step and movement you do in a day adds up to burn more calories. You could even play the air drum or air guitar if you're a music fan if that's your type of thing.

Have Fun While You Exercise

If you're not a professional athlete trying to build a specific body type, any exercise will do you good. Dancing, walking, swimming, or playing with your kids, all count as exercise. There is no need to pay for expensive gym memberships, which you may use infrequently if you find that the gym is not really for you.

Don't think of exercise as punishment after you eat "forbidden food" or as a way of losing weight, but as a fun activity with possible great health benefits. It can help your heart get stronger, build muscles, and get you out of the house. If you exercise regularly, you're also less likely to crave unhealthy foods, as exercise can help you control your stress levels.

Fun Ways To Exercise Without Exercising

There are many fun things you can do to get exercise and relieve your stress at the same time.

- Hiking is a great way to get out of your house and explore the world. Go with family or friends and have fun while getting much-needed exercise in the open air. Just make sure you wear the right shoes and that you're comfortable.

- If you don't have time for hiking, walking will also do. Even short walks of a few minutes at a time can get you closer to your goal of becoming fit and healthier. Other idea to spend less time sitting at work is to go for standing and walking meetings.

- If you're quite fit already, rock climbing might be the option that gets you out of the house. It's a great way of working out your arms/back and forearms. You'll also feel proud of yourself when you get to the top of the wall, and the climbing routes are graded so that you can choose more challenging ones as you get fitter and stronger.

- If you're keen on dancing, it's a great way to elevate your heart rate and sweat your stress away. Doesn't it sound fun to learn exotic dances like Zumba or Flamenco?

- Martial arts could be a great way to have fun and get fit. Honestly, people will also think you're pretty badass if you can master kung fu or karate.

- Cleaning your house can also be good exercise, although most of us don't like doing it all that much. But it's possible to make a game out of it to make it more fun. Put music at full blast while dancing and singing along when you clean your house. Listen to podcasts while you wash your windows, the dishes, or your car. After a few songs, you'll just keep on going.

- Handstands and cartwheels are a fun way of building your arm and core strength. However, make sure you're in good enough health and won't end up hurting yourself before trying some of these moves. So go to the park, by yourself or with your kids, and do some cartwheels, handstands, somersaults, or whatever else will make you feel young again.

- If you prefer gentle exercise and want to relax, try to do some yoga. Yoga can also help you build flexibility and strength. There are many kinds of yoga, and you'll need to find the kind that best suits your needs. Try out a few different styles and see what offers you the best option.

- Go and play at your local playground, go down the slide, balance on the balance beam, or swing across the monkey bars.

- Ride your bicycle to work. Not only will you save money, but you'll also get a great workout. It's also possible to do it with friends and family members.

- Basic, everyday movements that we do as part of our day can also push up our exercise total. When you go somewhere in your car, park at the far end of the parking lot. Take the stairs at work. It can be tiring at first, but it will soon become a healthy routine.

- Finally, this might sound strange and feel strange at first, but fidget more. Move every part of your body, from tapping your toes to music to getting up at your desk and sitting back down again. Pace around your office. Think back to your childhood when fidgeting was natural to you.

Key Takeaways

- Exercise can benefit your physical health, but the trick is to find a type of exercise you enjoy doing. It doesn't have to be something formal like going to the gym. Just moving more in your house, or cleaning your home, can already help you burn calories. Many people struggle to keep to an exercise routine because they don't enjoy doing it.

- You can start exercising at any age, even if you've never done any exercise before. However, first speak to your doctor to ensure that your health is good enough to start exercising, especially if you're already a bit older. It's also safest to increase your level of exercise only gradually.

- Exercise has some long-term benefits that can be very beneficial for your health. It lowers your risk of developing serious conditions like heart disease and diabetes and strengthens your bones and muscles. It also has fantastic short-term benefits, and it's often easier to motivate yourself to keep going by keeping these benefits in mind.

- Exercise is also a fantastic mood booster. When you exercise, your body releases chemicals that will improve your mood and make you feel relaxed. The stress of your day will just flow away, and your risk of developing depression will also drop quite a bit.

- The best way to get fit is to compile a weekly workout program that focuses on different components of fitness. This can help you get fit in almost no time and also reduces the risk of getting yourself injured.

- "Cardio" makes your heart beat faster and gets your entire system going. If you're a beginner, you could start by doing short, fast walks every day outside or on your treadmill at home, if you own one, or in the gym. You could also walk for 5 to 10 minutes a few times a day. Short bits of exercise add up at the end of the day or week and can also improve your overall fitness and health.

- Cardio exercise, such as running, swimming, cycling, rowing, or using exercise machines, is really good for you, as it will make your heart beat faster, which gets more oxygen into your body and circulates it to your muscles. Swimming is regarded as one of the best forms of exercise, as it is also an overall body workout.

- If you choose to start with light to moderate exercise and want to start jogging, you could start off slowly by jogging for a few minutes and then walking for a few minutes. Keep alternating the exercises until you feel fit enough to jog or run full out. At first, you can walk for a few minutes and then jog for 30 to 60 seconds.

- Exercise can help you get fit and even lose weight in the process, although this shouldn't be your primary goal. You have to find a type of exercise that you really enjoy, and that helps you create a daily routine that you can follow.

- Even moving around in your home or at your office can help you burn calories throughout the day. It's not good for your health to sit all day long, so make sure you get on your feet, even if you just pace around your office or go for a short walk outside. While sitting down, try to move some of your body parts frequently, for example, your hands and feet or your fingers and toes.

- For some people, this is difficult but try not to think of exercise as punishment after you eat "forbidden food" or as a way of losing weight. Instead, you should see it as a fun activity with possible health benefits that can make you stronger and get you out of the house. You could even improve your physical appearance by building muscle tone.

- Try yoga if you enjoy gentle exercise that can help you relax. Yoga can also help you build flexibility and strength. There are many different kinds of yoga, and you need to try out the other options to find the one that best suits your needs and health requirements.

- The everyday movement that we do as part of our day can also push up our exercise total. You can boost your exercise total for the day by parking at the far end of the parking lot, wherever you go. Take the stairs at work. These additional bits of exercise can be tiring at first, but they can soon be part of a new healthy routine.

- Try fidgeting to get yourself moving. Move every part of your body, from pacing up and down to wriggling your toes and fingers. Don't sit too long in one position, but constantly move around.

Chapter 3:

Imagine To Win

Imagination can help you get to a better place in your life. It makes you realize while you're down now, you're certainly far from out. Imagination can help you solve something which might seem like a crisis in a creative way and turn it into an opportunity. This is also the difference between imaginative people and those negative people who see themselves as being stuck in their daily reality and unable to change it. Those of us who can imagine ourselves in a better position will never be victims of our circumstances, as we will find ways to get ahead, even if we face obstacles that appear impossible to overcome to other people.

Why Is Imagination Important and How Should You Use Yours?

As we get older, we may wish that we could return to childhood to miss out on experiencing some of the stresses of adult life. Adult life is often full of thorns and is not as bright, cheerful, and fun as when we were children.

One of the reasons why children are able to have so much fun and enjoy their lives is because of the way they see the world. They often live in imaginary, fantastical worlds. They interact with friendly and cute characters who are always kind to them. Their fertile imaginations often take them to lands that adults can't comprehend any longer.

What Is Imagination?

Imagination is our ability to explore and think about ideas and concepts that might not be part of our current lives. We can imagine things that we really want for ourselves or even the direction we want our lives to go in general.

Interestingly, there are two types of imagination, namely Synthetic and Creative. Synthetic Imagination occurs when someone mixes their life experiences and existing ideas with imaginary concepts. Creative imagination can be described as the process of thinking like a child and using that ability to see something that doesn't exist at the present time.

Children don't know the difference between logical and illogical thinking. Adults tend to become forced into logical thinking as they want to be one of the group and don't want to be left out or seen as different. This limits our imagination, and as adults, we often struggle to see that logic is limiting. In contrast, imagination can take us anywhere, and we can even use it to reshape our universe.

Why Is Imagination Necessary To Lead Successful Lives?

One of the first steps to a successful and happy future is to imagine it. An abundance of imagination can help you change your present life, especially if you're unhappy with it. You'll often find those pessimistic people are so immersed in their current lives that they don't have the capacity to imagine a better future. They never seem to solve anything, and their life is an endless spiral of continuing trouble.

Optimistic people have the ability to look past their present troubles and see themselves living happy and prosperous lives in the future. Their fertile imaginations allow them to build and live the lives they want to live.

Our fear of failure can also often prevent us from imagining a better life for ourselves. If we're always only striving to overcome challenges, we lose the ability to be passionate about life and its possibilities, and our only priority becomes our survival.

The Magic of Imagination

Children have the ability to change their lives into something magical by using their imagination. A cardboard box can become a rocket or even a castle while your child is a prince or a knight. Think of ways you can incorporate your childhood imagination into your adult life. You can still enjoy a more fun and creative life while still being responsible for your life as an adult.

Thinking Outside The Box

A great benefit of imagination is that it can help you think outside the box when it comes to your career and even your personal life. We're always so worried about money and meeting our responsibilities that we don't continuously evolve mentally as we should. Thinking out of the box and finding more creative and easier ways of doing things can help you get ahead in life.

Using Your Imagination

Your imagination will come into play when your mind is relaxed, and you're able to have pleasant thoughts. There are ways that you can boost your imagination.

Daydreaming is an excellent way to let your imagination run free, but don't interrupt it with electronic devices such as computers or mobile phones. You can even make it a priority and set time for yourself to daydream daily in a bid to get closer to your happy and successful future.

Taking part in new activities can also boost your imagination. Do something to get yourself out of your boring routine and start taking part in new activities such as painting or baking.

Observe the world around you and let it stimulate your imagination. Small things, such as the feeling of the cold wind against your warm skin, the taste of an exotic fruit, or the smell of your coffee, can stimulate your creativity. Just ask any writer where they get the small details that make the environment in their books seem so realistic.

Getting involved in new art forms can also get your creativity going. Maybe you think you won't be good enough, or you don't have an artistic bone in your body, but you'll be surprised how practicing new art skills can unleash your creativity.

Try to take a break from your modern gadgets and electronics, and you'll find that this will boost your imagination even more.

Using The Power of Your Imagination To Overcome Stress

When you were a child and life wasn't going your way, your imagination probably provided you with a safe haven and a way to block out some of the scary realities of the world.

Imagination has great benefits for the development of children, but it doesn't have to stop as we age. As adults, we can use our imaginations to reduce our stress levels. It can help us solve problems and help us develop more characteristics and abilities to deal with life's challenges.

Guided Imagery

Guided imagery techniques can help us create images and sensations in our minds to help us relax.

The following techniques can help you get started when it comes to addressing your stress levels:

Safe Place Visualization

This technique is part of meditation and also mindfulness practices. When you're anxious or stressed, close your eyes and imagine yourself in a safe place. This will help you feel calm and more positive.

Imagining natural scenes and environments can also help you reduce your stress levels.

When you're stressed, try to go to a quiet place, close your eyes and imagine yourself in one of your favorite places in nature, such as the beach, mountains, or at a lake. Imagine this place as vividly as you can by using all your senses.

The Lightstream Technique

Make sure you're in a quiet space, and then start to consider if you're experiencing any disturbing bodily sensations. Try to think of any characteristics that could embody this sensation, such as texture, color, and size. Do you associate a certain color with this feeling?

Now, start to imagine a light of the color that you chose forming at the top of your head and begin visualizing the light beaming through your body to your feet.

The light will target the shape of the disturbing bodily sensation and change shape as it sinks and reverberates through it. Can you imagine how the shape, size, color, and intensity change? Allow this healing light to continue working its way through other unpleasant sensations in your body.

Evocative Imagery

It's also possible to manage your stress levels by using creative visualization and evocative imagery.

Begin by identifying qualities and personal characteristics you would like to develop. For example, maybe you want to be kinder, more confident, or more patient. Now, imagine these qualities starting to form in your body and become stronger.

Imagine the kind of person you would be if you had all these qualities and envision how you would handle certain challenges while you model these characteristics.

Keep on feeling these qualities in your body, see them as colors and tones and let them reverberate through your body. Continue imagining how you might use them in your day-to-day decisions, your relationships, and other interactions with the world. As you practice letting these qualities play out in your mind, you'll find yourself acting more in line with these qualities in your daily life.

Thought Diffusing

We all have those negative thoughts that seem to come automatically from time to time. If you don't manage these thoughts, they could worsen your anxiety and stress.

When these thoughts come to you, imagine them as autumn leaves that are falling from a tree. Watch as they drift away, fall into a stream, and are then washed away.

Your imagination could heighten your stress levels, but at the same time, it could also help you become more mentally clear.

Interactive Element: Visual Imagery

If you're going to use these techniques to reduce your stress levels, you will create a detailed mental image of a peaceful and attractive environment and setting. Guided imagery is often used together with physical relaxation techniques such as massage and progressive muscle relaxation.

The guided imagery technique will help you relax, as it will take your attention away from what is stressing you and aim it at an alternative focus.

One of the goals of guided meditation is to teach you to detach yourself from the contents of your mind so that you can watch your thoughts streaming through your mind almost as an independent observer.

There is no single correct way that you can use visual imagery to provide you with stress relief, but the following steps can help you get started:

- Make sure you are comfortable in a calm and private space

- Take slow and deep breaths to calm yourself and focus your attention.

- Close your eyes and imagine yourself in a beautiful location, such as a mountain, a forest, or wherever else you enjoy spending your time. You could even be sitting in your favorite comfortable chair at home.

- Imagine yourself as calm and relaxed or happy and having a good time.

- Focus on the sensory attributes in your scene to make it more real to you. For example, how the cold wind feels on your skin, the sand between your toes, how the ocean smells, and the sound seagulls make. The more you use your senses, the more vivid the image you can create will become.

- Stay in your scene for at least five to ten minutes or until you feel relaxed. While you're relaxed, tell yourself that you can return to this place whenever you want to relax.

Key Takeaways

- If you can imagine a better life for yourself, you'll never be a victim of your circumstances. You'll find ways to get ahead, and you'll be able to overcome obstacles that might seem impossible to other people.

- Children live in imaginary, fantastical worlds, which helps them have a great deal of fun and enjoy their lives. They simply see the world in a different light than adults.

- Imagination can help us explore and think about ideas and concepts we might not have in our current lives. For example, if you want to be a doctor, you must imagine yourself as one and what you should be doing to reach this goal.

- A child doesn't know the difference between logical and illogical thinking. As adults, we tend to become trapped by logical thinking as we want to be one of the group and don't want to be left out or seen as different. This limits our imagination. It's often difficult for adults to see that logic is limiting, while imagination can help us reshape our universe and can even make us believe that we're capable of doing so much more than we think.

- We need to imagine a successful and happy future before we can start taking the steps to get there.

- Optimistic people see themselves living as happy and successful people in the future. They can see past the challenges they face in their lives at the present time.

- Fear of failure can prevent some people from imagining better lives for themselves.

- If you use your imagination like a child, you could change your life into something magical.

- Imagination can help you think outside the box, significantly benefiting your career and your private life. You'll get so much further in life if you're able to see things from different perspectives.

- It's easier to be imaginative when your mind is relaxed and you're having pleasant thoughts.

- If you want to boost your imagination, get out of your boring routine, and start taking part in new activities. These can be creative activities such as painting and drawing.

- Involving yourself in new art forms can make you more creative. Try to approach this in a positive and self-confident way. Many people are scared to try artistic activities since they think they don't have a creative bone in their bodies.

- Taking a break from your electronic gadgets can also boost your imagination and your creative abilities.

- You can also reduce your stress levels by imagining natural scenes and environments.

- In times of stress, go to a quiet place, close your eyes and imagine yourself in one of your favorite places. This should preferably be a place in nature, such as the beach, mountains, or at a lake. Use all your senses to imagine this place as vividly as you can.

- You can also manage your stress levels by using creative visualization and evocative imagery.

- Imagine the type of person you want to be. Think about all the qualities and characteristics you need and how they would enable you to handle challenges.

- Follow the guide imagery technique to help you relax. It will take your attention away from what is stressing you and aim it at an alternative focus.

- Guided meditation can teach you to detach yourself from the contents of your mind. This will enable you to watch your thoughts streaming through your mind almost as if you are someone else, watching what is happening in your mind.

Chapter 4:

Express Yourself

I've always been able to express my emotions through food and dancing. I would find myself tapping my foot, dancing, or singing along to music when cooking. I enjoy indulging in the rituals of chopping, stirring, and tasting. There is nothing more enjoyable to me than cooking for my friends and family and seeing their happy faces light up as they enjoy the sumptuous food I cook. Being of Asian heritage, I was raised in a household full of different sauces and spices. Both my parents are amazing cooks, but my mother mostly dominated the kitchen. My happiest memories are of my parents' endless dinner parties, followed by dancing and karaoke for entertainment. I never really learned to cook until I left home to go to university to study nursing. I missed my mom's home-cooked meals so much that I started to explore and experiment with whatever ingredients I could find to recreate my mom's dinners. My attempts were satisfactory, but my Mama's cooking was always better!

As I got older and my life became full of responsibilities, I lost the opportunity to get creative with my cooking. Long and busy day and night nursing shifts didn't help. Gradually, I lost touch with myself, running between work and family life. I started to forget who I was and lost interest in my career. Every day seems to be just about surviving stress, paying bills, and making deadlines. I began to feel old and tired, like some essential part of my life was missing. Cooking became a necessity and felt like a chore rather than something I really enjoyed. My local takeaway restaurant was basically on my speed dial.

Then, one day, I watched a cooking show on TV where the cook was creating Asian-inspired meals, and a sudden feeling of inspiration came to me. I remembered how much I loved cooking nutritious meals and how amazing this made me feel. I realized how much I have neglected myself by frequently eating processed food, which was also probably why I felt so miserable. I started cooking again, and I am happy I did, as I have rediscovered that I am in a much calmer and less frazzled mood when I cook, and cooking for others was something I really missed. Not to mention the confidence boost I get from the praise I receive.

Creative Self-Expression

Having some form of creative expression in your life can be an excellent outlet for overwhelming thoughts and feelings. Some people may prefer to express their thoughts and feelings by writing in journals, creative stories, or poetry. However, if you're more of a visual person, you could also prefer to express yourself through painting, drawing, or photography.

This type of self-expression involves activities where you transfer the energy from your potentially negative thoughts and feelings into another form. This could make us feel better.

The Benefits of Self-Expression

When you get to express your feelings honestly in some way, you can deal with them better, as you know what you're feeling, instead of denying it. You need to let your feelings out somehow, as your stress and anxiety will get worse if you suppress negative emotions.

Our thoughts and ideas inhabit our bodies with energy. If this energy just sits there untouched, it can turn on itself, and you could start to feel anxious and restless. We need to express our creativity, to remain emotionally well.

Artistic activities can have many therapeutic benefits. They're a healthy form of escapism and can also free our unconscious minds. Coloring books for adults can be a healthy way to free your mind if you don't have other artistic forms of expression. When involved with activities like these, you could find that you go into a state of creative "flow" and become so focused on what you're doing that you lose all sense of time and self.

Putting our mental process into physical form helps us to be more in control of our thoughts and feelings, and we can understand them more clearly. Becoming involved in creative activities helps us externalize our thought processes and observe them from a distance, which means we don't have to act on our feelings impulsively.

Types of Creative Expression

Many of us wrongly believe that we're not creative and that only artists or writers possess this ability. However, anyone can really learn to be creative.

It's about tapping into your senses and expressing yourself from a place of deep connection.

You should be creative in whichever way you enjoy. It doesn't necessarily have to be something like painting or writing, but you can try out new recipes or even think outside the box to solve problems differently.

Also, it's healthier to focus on the process of being creative and not the end product.

Art therapy has been shown to help with mental health conditions such as anxiety, depression, schizophrenia, and other types of cognitive impairment.

The idea behind focusing on the end result and not the process is if we focus too much on the results, we start judging ourselves. For example, if you're a writer, you might criticize your early attempts at the finished masterpieces of well-known writers. This might make you give up before you really start at something.

Accepting what emerges from your creative process can be extremely healing. You become attuned to your creative impulses and let them emerge rather than trying to judge and suppress them.

Creative expression makes us heal, as it gives us somewhere to put our emotions. You'll find the most healing if you let your emotions flow and create something creative that can touch the heart of other people.

Mindful Creativity Can Teach Us Self-Expression

If you approach creativity mindfully, you'll be able to express yourself from a place of deep connection.

You connect to your experience on a deeper level when you meditate, and it's easier to find your authentic self in the creative process.

Let yourself become a conduit for creative energy. Writers, poets, and artists through the ages believed that they had to become channels for creativity, and they trusted their own output.

Taking part in activities outside your comfort zone can also get your creative juices flowing. If you don't know where to start, here are a few tips to get you going.

Drawing is helpful in encouraging more creativity, and you can express yourself by drawing informal shapes and using whatever colors you love. Draw big, empty circles on paper and use markers and colored pencils to color them. Just draw whatever comes to you, use whatever colors inspire you, and see what happens when you start drawing.

Continue doing this until your paper is covered in different shapes and colors.

Writing prompts can encourage you to unleash your creativity. You'll be able to find many free resources with writing prompts online, and you can try these prompts for your journal writing or simply to get to know yourself better.

If you're a more extroverted person who thrives on social interaction, your creativity can be further enhanced by finding a creative community. Try to find groups where the members aren't too judgmental, and you can share in the work of others and support each other. Finding a group or taking classes will also hold you accountable, especially if you have to meet deadlines.

If you get stuck in your creative endeavors, lower your standards and keep working on whatever project it is you hope to complete. Don't let perfectionism and being judgmental toward yourself hold you back.

Expressing Yourself Through Humor

Humor can get us through tough situations in life. People who can crack a joke during stressful situations usually deal well with whatever life throws at them, and they can get through the difficulties of day-to-day life.

Humor just has the capacity to improve our lives on so many levels.

The long-term effects of humor can even strengthen our immune systems. The medical world has even started to take notice of how humor therapy can improve our health as it reduces the stress that can be associated with illness and disease.

There have been many theories on why we laugh and what triggers laughter. However, what's important in the end is that it triggers positive emotions such as hope, joy, a sense of well-being, and even confidence. Humor is also a positive way of coping, through which feelings of anger can even be diffused.

Humor can also be an excellent way to get rid of anxiety and fears, such as fear of the unknown, fear of failure, and fear of death.

Laughter has benefits for your body that you've probably never considered. Just imagine watching your favorite comedy series can help you stabilize your blood pressure, improve your digestion and stimulate your circulation. It increases the oxygen supply to your muscles which will help relieve your muscle tension and make you feel better overall.

Even some hospitals have humor programs for their patients, as it helps take patients' minds off their illness, making them less likely to become depressed.

The Benefits of Crying

When we were children, crying came naturally to us. However, as adults, we often feel too ashamed to cry, especially in public.

While many of us see it as a sign of weakness, crying is actually healthy for you. The Japanese even have "crying clubs" where people get together to watch tear-jerker movies and have a good sob. They believe crying releases stress and is a great way of staying mentally healthy.

Crying will also activate your parasympathetic nervous system and restore your body's balance. However, crying at work or during meetings could be seen as a sign of weakness. Rather, wait until you are in a private place, such as an office or empty bathroom stall, before you let the tears flow.

Having a healthy cry can ease your emotional and physical pain, as emotional tears release oxytocin and endorphins. This will reduce your physical pain and promote your emotional well-being.

Crying will reduce the stress hormones in your body and improve your mood. It could also help you sleep better, as the mood-enhancing and calming effects can help you fall asleep easier.

While crying can boost your physical and mental health, if you cry too frequently, it could be a sign that you're depressed. You could be depressed if you frequently cry or for no reason, and it starts to affect your daily activities.

Interactive Element: Creative Journaling

It's tempting to think that writers, painters, songwriters, and filmmakers have a never-ending source of creativity and are always able to produce their best work. However, even for the experts, it can be challenging to be creative at all times.

That's why, even if you're a seasoned creative, you need to have some kind of creative outlets, such as creative journaling. Journaling is an excellent way of boosting your confidence and can help you find unlimited inspiration.

Your journaling doesn't only have to involve writing words down on paper. A creative journal can contain diary entries, drawings, doodles, poems, and newspaper clippings.

Creative journaling can help you overcome inner resistance like writer's block. The first steps are just to start and keep going, even if you feel you're not completely ready. It will build your confidence because the more you do something, the more you'll also start to believe you can do something.

Creative Journaling Ideas

There are various ways you can express yourself through creative journaling.

Art/Creative Journal

You could follow a few different processes for this one and really unleash your creative juices.

You can use a sketchbook to draw or paint whatever you see around you or what comes to mind. There is no pressure or guidelines that you need to follow.

A coloring book can be healing for your mind. You can buy one with bubble letters, shapes, or outlines or even create some templates yourself.

You could also make a scrapbook with your favorite quotes, photos, or whatever you want to put in there.

An art journal gives you the option to mix art with a written element.

You could even write about your drawings, what the meaning is behind them, and why you've used particular images.

You can write about all kinds of things in your creative journal. If you're a writer, you could even write down plot inspirations or ideas for characters. If you write poetry, this is a good place where you can do it.

You could even write down or illustrate your favorite recipes in your journal.

If you're better at narrating your life aloud, you could keep a video journal.

Dream Journal

Keeping a dream journal can give you some deeper insight into yourself. Write down or sketch what you dreamed about the night before, even if you only remember certain snippets or images.

Travel Diaries

These are also good sources of creativity and can show you what you've already achieved in life. It will also help you remember experiences you might have otherwise forgotten.

You could even use it to store leftover coins and cash from the different countries you've visited. It's also a great place to store souvenirs such as concert tickets, flight reservations, or festival wristbands.

Planner

If you enjoy journaling, you could also use it to do daily or yearly planning. Write down your goals and plans and track your progress.

Decide which of these options appeals to you and start keeping your own journal.

Key Takeaways

- Creativity can be an excellent outlet for your overwhelming thoughts and feelings.

- When you get to express your feelings honestly in some way, you can deal with them better, as you recognize what you're feeling instead of denying it. You need to let your feelings out in some way. Stress and anxiety only get worse if you suppress your feelings.

- Artistic activities can have many therapeutic benefits, such as freeing our unconscious thoughts. They're also a wonderful form of escapism.

- Creative activities can help us externalize our thought processes and observe them from a distance, which means we don't have to act on our feelings impulsively. We can first analyze them and consider what steps we should take next.

- It's tempting to believe that only writers or artists possess the creative ability and use this as an excuse not to get involved in such activities. However, most of us can learn to be creative.

- While doing something creative, focus on the process, not the end product. This is also a good way of taking control of perfectionist tendencies. If you focus too much on the end product, you could also end up judging yourself if you feel what you've produced isn't good enough.

- Art therapy can help with mental health conditions such as anxiety, depression, schizophrenia, and other types of cognitive impairment.

- It can be very healing to accept the outcome of your creative process. Let your emotions flow and create something that allows you to reach other people and touch your hearts.

- An excellent way to get your creative juices flowing is to participate in activities outside your comfort zone.

- Humor can help us deal with tough situations. People who regularly crack jokes during stressful situations usually deal well with whatever life throws at them, and they can get through the difficulties of day-to-day life.

- Humor can help you get rid of your anxieties and fears. For example, it can help you deal with a fear of the unknown, fear of failure, and fear of death.

- Laughter has important benefits for your body. For example, watching your favorite comedy series can help you stabilize your blood pressure, improve your digestion and stimulate your circulation. Laughing can also increase the oxygen supply to your muscles which will help relieve your muscle tension and just make you feel better overall.

- Crying will activate your parasympathetic nervous system and restore your body's balance. However, if you get the urge to cry while at work, wait until you're in a safe and private place. There is often a tendency to judge people for being weak when they cry in public.

- Crying can improve your mood and reduce your body's stress hormone.

- Crying can boost your physical and mental health. However, if you cry too frequently, it could be a sign that you're depressed.

- We may think writers, painters, songwriters, and filmmakers have a never-ending source of creativity and are always able to produce their best work. However, even for these experts, it can be challenging to be creative at all times.

- A creative journal doesn't always only have to consist of written words on paper. Your journal can contain diary entries, drawings, doodles, poems, and newspaper clippings.

- Coloring books for adults are great for releasing stress or practicing your creativity. You can buy one with different shapes or create your own templates.

- One of the most valuable benefits of keeping a dream journal is that it can give you an insight into your mind.

Chapter 5:

Rest & Sleep

If you are anything like me, your sleeping patterns have probably changed through the years. When I'm relaxed, I can sleep peacefully, for hours on end, like a growing teenager. During times of stress, I sleep more like a restless newborn who wakes up for every little thing.

I've always been an early bird. I am awake at the crack of dawn and could get a lot done during the first part of the day, but working night shifts was something my body refused to get used to. I remember clocking into work at 8 pm for my first night shift of three and dreading what was ahead. It was not so much about the workload but the relentless battle of staying awake. Just like clockwork, at around 10 pm, I would feel my body starting to long for my bed. I would start to relax and yawn, and my eyes would feel heavy as I sat through the handover. I would have to drink countless cups of coffee to stay awake and alert through extremely busy or, worse, through excruciatingly uneventful night shifts. After my 13-hour shift, I would drag myself home and climb into bed. I would fall asleep as soon as my head hit the pillow, but my body usually didn't allow me to sleep for more than a few hours. I would toss and turn, getting incredibly frustrated with my body's refusal to rest and sleep. Finally, I would get up and get ready for the next shift. With stinging eyes and a sleep-deprived body, I clocked in for another 13-hour shift. I have tried different hacks to get better sleep, from having a completely dark room to playing low-fi white noise. I even tried to give up drinking coffee. Insane, I know, but nothing worked.

It became apparent that I would never get used to night shifts, so I decided to leave the shift work and joined the 9 to 5 club. I am glad I did, as having a consistent sleep schedule has given me renewed energy and productivity. I am less irritable and able to regulate my emotions better.

Why You Need Sleep

Sleep allows you to recharge, and if you've had a good night's sleep, you should wake up refreshed and alert. If you don't sleep enough, you'll struggle to concentrate, remember things, and think clearly. If you don't get enough sleep for a long period, your risk of becoming seriously ill also increases.

As an adult, you need about seven to nine hours of sleep a night, but a hectic work schedule, medical conditions, or other stresses could prevent you from getting enough sleep.

A healthy diet and lifestyle habits can also help you sleep enough, but if you struggle to sleep in the long term, it could indicate a sleep disorder.

Your Internal Body Clock

Your internal body clock controls when you feel tired and when you're alert and awake. This clock has a 24 hour-cycle known as your circadian rhythm. After you wake up from a good night's sleep, you'll get increasingly tired throughout the day, leading up to your eventual bedtime.

The level of light can also affect your circadian rhythm. The nerve cells in your brain, which are known as the hypothalamus, as well as a cluster of cells that forms part of this, called the suprachiasmatic nucleus, process signals when your eyes are exposed to artificial or natural light. These signals can help your brain determine whether it's day or night.

When natural light starts to lessen toward the evening, your body will release melatonin, the hormone that will make you drowsy. When the sun rises again in the morning, your body will release cortisol, making you more energetic and alert.

Sleep Stages

Once you're asleep, your body will follow a sleep cycle that is divided into four stages. The first three stages are non-rapid eye movement (NREM) sleep, while the final stage is known as rapid eye movement (REM) sleep.

- Stage 1 is the transition from being awake to when you fall asleep, and this is known as light sleep. Your muscles will relax, your heart rate, breathing, and eye movements will slow down, and your brain waves will also slow. Stage 1 can last for several minutes.

- Stage 2 is a phase of even deeper sleep as your heart rate and breathing slow down further, and your muscles relax more. Your eyes will stop moving, your body temperature will decrease, and your brain waves will remain slow. This is usually the longest of the four sleep stages.

- Stage 3 is essential when it comes to making you feel alert and refreshed the next day. Your heartbeat, breathing, and brain wave activity will now reach their lowest levels, and your muscles will be completely relaxed.

- REM sleep: You will experience the first stage of REM sleep 90 minutes after you fall asleep. Your eyes will move back and forth rapidly under your eyelids. Your breathing rate, heart rate, and blood pressure will increase too. You can dream during REM sleep, and your arms and legs will be paralyzed. This happens to prevent you from acting out your dreams. The REMS sleep cycles become longer as the night progresses. Your REM sleep cycles will decrease as you get older.

Unfortunately, it seems you can develop a tolerance to chronic sleep deprivation. Your brain and body may be struggling due to a lack of sleep, but you might not even be aware of this since less sleep has started to feel normal to you. A lack of sleep can put you at higher risk of disease and medical conditions like obesity, type 2 diabetes, heart disease, stroke, and poor mental health.

If you feel you're not getting enough sleep, you can make some lifestyle changes to make sure you get more:

- Set yourself a bedtime and make sure you keep to it, even on weekends.

- Make sure your bedroom has a comfortable temperature since you could struggle to fall asleep if you're too hot or too cold. Your bedroom should also not be too light.

- Do some exercise during the day, as this can help you sleep better at night.

- Make sure your bed is comfortable and you have a comfortable mattress, pillows, and sheets.

- Try to limit your screen time, especially in your bedroom.

- Don't use coffee or alcohol too close to your bedtime.

Good Reasons To Get More Sleep

If you don't get enough sleep, you can be cranky the next day. However, there are multiple reasons why your body needs a good night's sleep:

- If you get enough sleep, your memory will be sharper, and you'll find it easier to remember details. Sleep plays an essential part in learning and memory, and you'll struggle to focus without enough sleep.

- Your brain also needs enough sleep to be able to process your emotions. You'll have more negative emotional reactions when you don't get enough sleep. If you have a chronic lack of sleep, it increases the probability that you can develop a mood disorder. People who struggle with insomnia are five times likelier to develop a mood disorder and anxiety and panic disorders.

- Your blood pressure also goes down while you sleep, which gives your heart and blood pressure a break. If you get less sleep, your blood pressure will stay elevated for longer in a 24-hour cycle.

- If you get sufficient sleep, your blood sugar levels will also be under better control, as the amount of glucose in your blood drops, during the deep, slow-wave part of your sleep cycle. If you don't spend enough time in this deep sleep cycle, it means you don't get enough of that break to have sufficient rest, and your body will struggle to respond to your cells' needs and blood sugar levels. If you're in a deep sleep longer, you're also less likely to develop type 2 diabetes later in life.

- A lack of sleep can affect the way your immune cells work. They could work less effectively, and you could fall ill more often. When you're sleep-deprived, you also tend to eat more, as the hormones that control your appetite, leptin, and ghrelin, are disturbed. You're less likely to crave unhealthy, fatty food, and when you're exhausted, you won't feel like getting up and moving around. So even if you hit the gym regularly, it will be challenging to manage your weight if you don't get enough sleep.

Why The Quality of Your Sleep Is Important

If you have trouble falling and staying asleep or going into deep REM sleep, you may also face similar issues to those people who aren't getting enough sleep.

If you want to figure out if you're getting quality sleep or not, ask yourself the following questions:

- Do you fall asleep in 30 minutes or less?

- Are you asleep most of the time you're in bed?

- If you wake up during the night, is it for 20 minutes or fewer?

- Do you wake up once or more during the night?

Another way to improve the quality of your sleep is to implement some relaxing activities before you go to bed, like having a warm bath or reading a book. You're more likely to struggle to fall asleep if you engage in high-energy or stressful activities before you fall asleep.

Healthy people need about 62 to 110 minutes of deep sleep a night. As you get older, though, you won't need as much deep sleep. While in deep sleep, most of your body's physical recovery will occur.

If you don't get enough deep sleep, your body can't recover, and you'll start getting symptoms of sleep deprivation.

Fragmented sleep can affect the quality of your sleep. That happens when you wake up for short times during the night and struggle to fall asleep again. You can usually remember waking up, and this reduces your total sleep time, making you feel tired the next day.

Certain sleep disorders can lead to fragmented sleep:

Sleep-Maintenance Insomnia

While you don't struggle to fall asleep, you're unable to sleep through the night. Sleep onset insomnia happens when you struggle to fall asleep.

Sleep Apnea

You tend to wake up from upper airway obstruction and oxygen desaturation.

Narcolepsy

Narcolepsy could also cause hallucinations, vivid dreams, and even paralysis for a short time when you fall asleep or wake up.

Sleep Chronotypes

We usually talk about night owls or early birds when we refer to sleep chronotypes. However, most people fall in between these types.

Your chronotype will also show how alert you feel at certain types of the day and will explain why you feel sleepier at other times.

Your sleep chronotype is related to your circadian rhythm, which controls your sleep-wake cycle.

Your chronotype may determine how productive you are during certain times of the day. If you're a natural night owl, you may wake up at 7 am, but you don't become productive until later in the day. If you're an early bird, you might be bright and awake during the early morning shift, but you already start to get sleepy in the late afternoon.

If you're an early bird, it'll be easier for you to get the recommended seven to nine hours of sleep a night. Night owls often find it difficult to fall asleep before 1 am, and they can struggle to adapt to work schedules.

It's difficult and almost impossible to change your natural sleep chronotype. If you are a night owl, you may suffer from what is called social jetlag and feel permanently tired if you have to wake up early for work or school. If you're an early bird, you might not do well with cultural or social activities that take place late at night.

What Determines Your Chronotype?

Your age, genetics, and even your geographical location can determine your chronotype.

Children mainly have an early chronotype, but this gets pushed back to later when they're teenagers, which could cause them to have difficulty waking up early for school in the morning. Chronotype then shifts earlier again from the age of 20. In middle age, we usually do best with a bedtime between 11 pm and 12 am, and then as we get older, the chronotype tends to shift earlier again.

If you want to figure out what type your chronotype is, think about when you want to wake up on days you have no other commitments. Read more below to discover your animal chronotype. People are usually divided into four chronotype categories: the wolf, the bear, the dolphin, and the lion.

The Bear

This type follows the solar cycle and doesn't struggle to fall asleep or wake up. The bear is most productive during mornings and typically sleeps up to eight hours, usually between 11 pm and 7 am.

If Bears don't get enough sleep, they'll feel tired throughout the day and go to bed earlier than usual. Bears are usually extroverts and get their energy from conversations.

The Wolf

The wolf is mostly productive at night and usually needs to sleep longer in the mornings. They typically have the most creative energy at noon and around 6 pm when others usually finish their work for the day. Wolves usually only go to bed past midnight and may have difficulty getting up in the mornings. Wolves are usually more introverted.

The Lion

The lion usually has a lot of energy in the morning, and they find it easy to wake up and get going. However, they start to run out of steam by midday.

They could need a nap to recharge and may end up feeling drained by the evening. Lions need to implement a wind-down routine before they go to bed.

Lions are usually type-A people, and they are charismatic leaders.

Dolphins

Dolphins are insomniacs who stay alert, even while they're asleep. They usually struggle to get going in the morning, and they are at their most productive, usually around mid-morning.

Dolphins can have underlying tiredness as a result of their anxious sleeping behavior. They struggle to fall asleep and often don't get a full night of sleep.

Dolphins can be distant during social interactions.

Interactive Element: Chronotype Quiz

The quiz below can give you a hint of what chronotype you are. Answer the questions as honestly as you can. Don't take it too seriously, and compare your answers to the chronotype information in the paragraphs above.

Do sounds or lights keep you up?

Do you wake up before your alarm rings or only after it rings?

Can you sleep on planes? Do you need an eye mask and earplugs to sleep?

I often get irritable because I'm tired during the day.

A doctor diagnosed me as an insomniac.

I tend to worry about the small things in life.

Are you a perfectionist?

Were you anxious about your grades in school?

Do you lay awake at night, thinking about what happened in the past and worrying about what may still happen in the future?

If you don't have anything important to do the next day, at what time would you wake up?

- Before 6:30 a.m.

- Between 6:30 a.m. and 8:45 a.m.

- After 8:45 a.m.

When do you wake up during the weekends?

- The same time as during the workweek.

- 45 to 90 minutes past your workweek schedule.

- 90 minutes or more after your schedule in the week.

What's your favorite meal of the day? Breakfast, lunch, or dinner?

At what time do you concentrate the best during the day? Early morning, early afternoon, or during the midafternoon?

At what time of the day would you prefer to do an intense workout?

- Before 8:00 a.m.

- From 8:00 a.m. to 4:00 p.m.

- After 4:00 pm.

If you could choose your own work hours, which hours would you work?

- 4:00 a.m. to 9:00 a.m.
- 9:00 a.m. to 2:00 p.m.
- 4:00 p.m. to 9:00 p.m.

Do you think of yourself as a logical, analytical, or creative thinker?

Do you ever take naps?

Do you make healthy choices when it comes to exercise and healthy eating, or do you struggle?

Are you comfortable with taking risks?

Are you awake or still sleepy when you get up in the morning?

Do you tend to live in the present, future, or past?

Do you suffer from insomnia?

How is your overall life satisfaction?

Key Takeaways

- Sleep recharges us, and you should wake up alert if you've had a good night's sleep. If you don't sleep enough, you'll struggle to concentrate and think clearly. Your memory will also suffer. If you don't get enough sleep for a long period, your risk of becoming seriously ill also increases. Chronic sleep deprivation will also have a negative effect on your mood.

- Adults need about seven to nine hours of sleep a night. A hectic work schedule, medical conditions, or other stresses could prevent you from getting enough sleep.

- If you're having a long-term struggle with sleep, it could indicate a sleep disorder.

- Your internal body clock controls when you feel tired and when you're alert and awake. This clock has a 24 hour-cycle, which is known as your circadian rhythm. When you wake up in the morning, you'll become gradually more tired throughout your day, leading up to your bedtime.

- Your body's sleep cycle is divided into four stages. The first three stages are non-rapid eye movement (NREM) sleep, while the final stage is known as rapid eye movement (REM) sleep.

- Many people end up developing a tolerance to chronic sleep deprivation. While they might be struggling physically and mentally because of a lack of sleep, they might not notice it, as it has become normal to them.

- It's possible to make lifestyle changes or changes to your environment in an effort to get more sleep.

- Your memory will be sharper, and you'll find it easier to remember details when you get enough sleep. Sleep plays an essential part in learning and memory. You'll find it nearly impossible to focus at work or in class if you're not getting enough sleep.

- You also need to get enough sleep for your brain to be able to process your emotions. Your emotional reactions will be negative if you're not getting the rest your body needs. A chronic lack of sleep even increases the probability of developing a mood disorder. Those of us who struggle with insomnia are five times more likely to develop a mood disorder, and we're also at risk of anxiety and panic disorders.

- If you struggle to fall and stay asleep and you don't get enough REM sleep, you may also face similar issues to people who don't get enough sleep.

- You can also improve the quality of your sleep by implementing relaxing activities before you go to bed, like having a warm bath or reading a book.

- Fragmented sleep can affect the quality of your sleep. That happens when you wake up for short times during the night and struggle to fall asleep again. If you wake up but don't remember this the following day, it will usually not affect your sleep.

- If you're an early bird, you'll find getting the recommended seven to nine hours of sleep a night relatively easy. Night owls often only fall asleep in the early hours of the morning, and they can find it difficult to adapt to work schedules.

- It's difficult and almost impossible to change your natural sleep chronotype. If you are a night owl, you may suffer from what is called social jetlag and feel permanently tired if you have to wake up early for work or school. Early birds often don't do well at social events that are scheduled to take place late at night.

Chapter 6:

Mindful Pause

Do you rush through your days between work, managing your children and household, as well as other activities?

You may think you don't have any time to take breaks or pauses, but the reality is that you will perform better at work and in your personal life if you take regular breaks to refresh your body and mind.

Living in a state of constant chaos will only cause you to make more mistakes at work and can also hurt the relationships in your life.

Taking pauses throughout your day can also benefit your health, and you'll be able to make better decisions when it comes to taking care of yourself.

The Power of Pause

Do you feel like your life is full of noise and chaos? Our culture is fast-paced and ever-changing, and it may seem like there is never time to take a break. Introverts may especially find this overwhelming and could end up wishing that they could just stop time or slow life down. Unfortunately, the world won't slow down because you want it to do so, but you can make time to take pauses or breaks.

Taking a break from the frantic activity and noise can refresh and re-energize you. Your nervous system can regain its sense of balance when you give it time to be quiet and relax. You will also find that you perform better after taking breaks when you've had periods of intense activity.

If you want to allow your mind to recover, you need to consider the two types of noise.

Two Types of Noise

These are the two main types of noise:

- Outer noise is the noise you will typically hear from your environment around you. This could be anything from people talking to alarms going off. We're over-stimulated with outer noise, as you will experience noise 24/7 in most places. Many of us have also been conditioned to need constant noise and entertainment, and noise has simply become part of our culture.

- Inner noise can be described as the voice in your head that is constantly telling you what to do. Your mind continually bounces around from one thought to another, and your mind is soon flooded with constant chatter.

Taking a break from the outer noise is easy, as you can simply switch off your laptop or television. Quieting down your inner noise, however, is a little more challenging to do.

There are different things you can do to find your inner silence. A mindful pause can help you to check in with your emotions, principles, and feelings and can help you make better decisions for yourself.

Ways of Pausing

Taking a pause can help us be more present in the here and now. There are many benefits to pausing during your hectic day.

It helps you refocus and handle challenging moments better. If your brain is less cluttered with anxious thoughts, you'll be better able to solve problems. It also gives your nervous system the opportunity to regain its balance and will help you build stress resilience. It will allow you to shift your perspective to what's important.

Pausing can help you in many different situations, especially during stressful ones. The idea is to think and reflect on what you're going to do. Ask yourself questions, such as how the food you're about to eat will nourish your body.

Before doing an exercise, let go of all the thoughts floating around your head and focus on being present in the moment. While pausing, focus on your breathing and what your body can do.

Pauses are useful when you have to deal with stressful situations. It gives you time to take note of how you're feeling before dealing with these types of situations.

Taking a pause can also help you if you're having trouble getting a good night's rest.

Pause and focus on slowing your breathing to relax your busy mind.

You must also pause and ensure your environment is ready for quality sleep. Pause and try meditation to fall asleep if you're having trouble doing so.

Interactive Element: Guided Meditation and Deep Breathing Exercises

Deep breathing and guided meditation can calm your body and your mind.

Purposeful deep breathing can help you a great deal if you're anxious and stressed.

Deep breathing will help calm your sympathetic nervous system as changing your breathing to a slow, relaxed pattern helps your nervous system become calmer.

Breathing is also central to the different yoga variations.

How To Do Guided Meditation

You can practice guided meditation by sitting or lying in a comfortable environment. Listen to calming recordings when you practice your breathing.

The guided recording can help you visualize a calm reality. It can also help you control your anxiety-inducing thoughts. It interrupts your thinking patterns, which causes stress.

How To Practice Deep Breathing

Focus on your breathing and take long slow breaths from your stomach. You need to activate your sympathetic nervous system when you want to practice deep breathing. Close your eyes and imagine a stressful situation. Focus on how your body reacts. Does your heart beat faster? Are you breathing rapidly?

Focus on your breathing and breathe from your stomach. Count to three when you inhale and exhale. Do this for a while, even if you start feeling uncomfortable. You'll eventually notice that your body starts feeling more relaxed.

You'll need to find a way of practicing deep breathing that works best for you.

Try the following exercises:

Equal Breathing

Equal breathing means you're inhaling for the same amount of time you're exhaling. This breathing technique works best if you do it in a comfortable position, like when you're sitting or lying down. This technique is derived from the practice of pranayama yoga.

It's a simple process to perform:

Close your eyes and focus on the way you breathe.

Inhale through your nose, and count from one to four while doing this.

Focus on the fullness and emptiness of your lungs while you inhale and exhale.

Breathing Through Your Abdomen

You can reduce the work your body has to do when you breathe from your diaphragm.

Make sure you're in a comfortable position lying on a bed or the floor or sitting relaxed in a comfortable chair.

Put one of your hands under your rib cage and the other one over your heart.

Inhale and exhale through your nose and take notice of how your chest and stomach move while you're breathing.

Only your stomach should eventually move as you breathe, not your chest. You may find this tiring at first, but it will get easier the more you practice.

Resonant/Coherent Breathing

This technique can help you be less anxious and is easy to practice.

While lying down, breathe in through your nose for six seconds. Make sure you don't fill your lungs too much.

Breathe out slowly for six seconds and continue doing this for up to 10 minutes. Remain still for a bit longer and focus on how your body feels.

Lion's Breath

If you're going to do this technique, you need to kneel and cross your ankles while resting your bottom on your feet. Try sitting cross-legged, even if you don't find this comfortable.

Breathe through your nose while you put your hands on your knees and stretch your arms and fingers. When you breathe out through your mouth, vocalize "Ha." Open your mouth while you're exhaling and stick your tongue out toward your chin, as far as you can go.

Focus on the end of your nose while you exhale, relax your face and inhale again.

Breath Focus

Take notice of how your body feels when you inhale and exhale. Breathe through your nose, slowly and deeply. Your belly and upper body will expand. Do this for several minutes while you pay attention to how your stomach rises and falls.

Select a word you're going to say and focus on saying it while you exhale. Envisage the air you inhale, washing over you like a wave. Picture how this exhale carries away your negative energy and thoughts.

If you become distracted, focus on your breath and words. Try to practice this technique for 20 minutes a day when you're able to do so.

Key Takeaways

- You can re-energize yourself by taking a break from all the frantic activity and noise around you. Your nervous system will regain its balance if you allow it to be quiet and relaxed.

- The main types of noise are outer noise and inner noise.

- Outer noise is from the environment around you. This could be anything from people talking to alarms going off.

- Inner noise is to do with your inner voices that are constantly telling you what to do.

- Outer noise is manageable, as we can switch off our televisions, radios, and laptops. It's more complicated to quieten down inner noise.

- You can find your inner silence by taking a mindful pause. Pausing this way can help you check in with your emotions, principles, and feelings and help you make better decisions.

- Pausing also helps you refocus, which can help you manage challenging moments more effectively. Your problem-solving ability will improve if your brain isn't cluttered with anxious thoughts. Your nervous system will have an opportunity to regain its balance, and you can develop enhanced stress resilience. You will be able to shift your perspective to what's important.

- Pausing can help you in many different situations, especially during stressful ones. It's always helpful to think and reflect on what you're going to do.

- Pauses allow you time to take note of how you're feeling before dealing with different kinds of situations.

- Pausing and meditation can also help you fall asleep if you struggle to do so.

- Deep breathing and guided meditation can help you calm your body and mind.

- Deep breathing in a slow, relaxed pattern will help calm your sympathetic nervous system.

- You can practice guided meditation by sitting or lying in a comfortable environment. Listening to calming recordings can help your guided meditation be more relaxing.

Chapter 7:

Self-Compassion

I have always been the type of person others turn to if they want someone to listen to the challenges they face in their lives or when they seek a shoulder to cry on, or to get relief from some kind of catastrophe they had to face in their lives. While I'm compassionate toward others, I often struggle to treat myself with compassion. If I make a mistake, I can spend days agonizing over it. If I suspect I might have hurt someone's feelings or I made myself look ridiculous in a social setting, I usually feel even worse. I'm very hard on myself and find it difficult to forgive myself for any perceived wrongdoing.

This chapter looks at why it's also important to have compassion for yourself.

What Is Self-Compassion?

Having compassion for yourself is similar to having compassion for others.

Think about what it feels like to have compassion for others. You first need to notice that people are suffering to have compassion for them. If you ignore someone's suffering, you're unable to feel compassion for the difficulty of their experience.

If you have compassion for someone's suffering, you "suffer with" them and feel their pain. You'll feel caring and a desire to help the person who is suffering. Compassion also means you are understanding and kind to others when they make mistakes and when they fail at something without judging them. When you feel compassion for people rather than pity, it means you also understand that failure and imperfection are just part of the human experience.

Self-compassion means being kind to yourself when you are experiencing a difficult time or when you're experiencing setbacks and failures. What does this mean, though? It means not ignoring your pain and keeping a "stiff upper lip." Instead, you are kind to yourself and tell yourself, *"Things are difficult now, but I care about myself and can comfort myself."*

You may try to change some things about your lifestyle to make sure you're healthier and happier, but you do this because you care about yourself, not because you feel you're worthless or unacceptable.

You'll experience frustration, and your life won't always go how you want it to. This is the human condition for all of us.

Practicing Self-Compassion

Do you blame yourself when things go wrong in your life? Do you get angry with yourself?

We're often tougher on ourselves than we are on other people. However, this can just cause stress in our lives and even lead to us developing physical and mental health conditions. For our overall well-being, we need to forgive ourselves, accept our flaws, and show ourselves kindness. It can be more challenging than it sounds, but we can learn to make it a habit. Let's first take a look at the relationship we have with ourselves.

Our Relationship With Ourselves

Growing up, we're usually conditioned to see ourselves in certain ways through our interactions with our parents or other childhood caretakers. As a child, you might have modeled yourself after your caretakers and even adopted their values or ways of seeing and understanding the world.

We develop our guiding inner voice according to the environment we grow up in and the values we're taught during this time. Unfortunately, many people tend to develop a highly self-critical inner voice.

Most people have the tendency to take the values they grow up with, for example, expectations as to how they should perform. If their perceptions of their performance don't agree with their values, they'll judge themselves for being unworthy.

Our self-critical perceptions of whether we can live up to our values will impact our self-worth, which will, in turn, determine if our inner voices are kind and supportive or self-destructive.

The perception you have of yourself will also influence the way you behave. Unfortunately, this can mean that you live out a self-fulfilling prophecy, and you'll never measure up to your value of what is good enough.

It's important to make peace with your inner critic. Many people try to hide their shortcomings to ensure their self-images remain positive. If you treat yourself in a compassionate way, you can actually increase your knowledge and gain a better understanding of your own limitations.

Self-compassion can also help you improve your mental health and gain greater life satisfaction.

Techniques for Improving Your Self-Compassion

There are various steps you can use to improve your self-compassion:

Self-Kindness

Self-kindness is about still being kind to yourself even when you fail at something and not judging yourself when you are in pain.

Self-kindness is about treating ourselves as worthy, even when we fall short of our own expectations. We need to try and understand and be patient with our perceived personality flaws and be tolerant of our shortcomings.

Shared Humanity

It has always been argued that the need for connection is part of our human nature. A shared/common humanity means that we need to see our individual experiences as being embedded in the broader human experience and that we shouldn't see ourselves as being separate or isolated from others.

Another part of our shared or common humanity is realizing we're not alone when we feel hurt, and others can feel the same at times.

You should also see your shortcomings as being part of the human condition and view your difficulties as parts of life that other people go through as well. When you feel inadequate at times, you need to tell yourself that other people often also feel the same way.

Mindfulness

Mindfulness encourages self-compassion, as it will decrease your tendency to judge yourself. When being mindful, it's important to always be in the moment and to be aware of what's happening without judging yourself. Let yourself experience your thoughts and feelings at the moment, and then let them go.

Mindfulness involves acknowledging and labeling your thoughts and not only reacting to them.

When it comes to mindfulness being part of self-compassion, we're aware of our damaging thoughts and emotions without ruminating about them. Instead, we manage to adopt a balance between over-identification of our negative thoughts and emotions and avoiding them altogether.

Mindfulness also means keeping our feelings in balance when we go through an upsetting experience. Practicing mindfulness can also help us maintain our perspective when we fail at things that are important to us. It also allows us to better adapt to our emotions when we feel sad and pessimistic.

Another way to practice self-compassion is to develop a growth mindset. Whether you have a fixed or growth mindset can significantly impact your happiness.

Ask yourself this: Do you see challenges as obstacles that are almost impossible to overcome, or do you regard them as opportunities to grow?

Find meaning in the challenges you have to deal with rather than avoiding them. If you find you're comparing yourself to other successful people and judging yourself because you aren't there yet, try to find inspiration in their success instead of being threatened.

Feeling Gratitude

Feeling gratitude can make you feel better about yourself. Stop wanting things you don't have and appreciate the people and things you have in your life. One technique that works well is to keep a daily gratitude journal which helps you focus on your blessings. By doing this, your inner voice will also become gentler, and you'll focus less on your own shortcomings.

Take pauses to remind yourself that you're worthy of love. It's vital to forgive yourself when things go wrong and realize that you're only human. Accept that you are human and that you only did the best you could at the time. Maybe you could have done better, but what you did at the time is fine as well.

Reducing Self-Criticism

We have such busy lives today that it's often impossible to get everything done on our to-do lists. You may blame yourself for lack of time management and call yourself negative names, such as a "loser," or see yourself as too lazy to achieve your goals. However, it's crucial for your mental health to break this habit.

There are several things you can do to overcome your inner critic:

- Take note of how your self-criticism is impacting your mood and behavior. Write these thoughts down on paper or even jot them down on your phone.

- When you get these thoughts, determine what you're really saying to yourself. For example, when you call yourself a loser, identify what this term really means to you.

- Examine if there is evidence that your thoughts are really true. For example, have you *really* never succeeded at anything in your life, or aren't you looking at the full picture? You need to consider all the facts.

- Consider if you believe that your self-criticism is doing anything for you. Some people believe that their self-criticism serves as motivation.

- Make sure you have opportunities for success every day by setting achievable goals for yourself.

- Be honest when you consider the mistakes you've made in the past, but don't ruminate about them. Engage in self-correction and ask yourself how to learn and grow from past mistakes.

- When you notice that you're becoming self-critical, ask yourself if you would say the same thing to other people you care about. If you wouldn't do it, don't say it to yourself, either.

- When you achieve your goals for the day, say something positive to yourself or reward yourself with activities you enjoy, such as going for walks when you achieve your daily goals.

Challenging Your Negative Self-Talk

Our internal voice helps us determine how to perceive different situations. This voice is our "self-talk," and it includes our conscious thoughts and unconscious assumptions and beliefs.

Negative self-talk can make us feel angry and depressed. We could also start behaving in self-defeating ways. For example, if you think you're going to fail an exam, it might prevent you from studying hard and adequately preparing for the exams, which could then lead to you failing.

Positive self-talk will help you challenge negative thinking by replacing your unhelpful thoughts with more reasonable ones.

A particular challenge with negative self-talk is that the negative things you say to yourself might seem true to you. It's so tempting to assume that your negative thoughts are facts, while they are actually just based on your perceptions. When you're feeling down, your thoughts could be particularly harsh. There is no reason to doubt yourself, as you're capable of achieving much more than you think.

Negative self-talk is dangerous to your self-esteem. When you're depressed, you'll be tough on yourself, judging and criticizing yourself. Your self-talk will become more negative the worse you feel. It could help your self-talk to try to see things in a more positive light. Challenge your negativity by imagining a friend in your situation and think about what you'll say to them. We're usually nicer to our friends than we are to ourselves.

Challenging the negative aspects of your thinking can help you respond to challenges in a more helpful way. When you find yourself starting to think in a negative way, consciously decide to think about the situation in a more realistic way. You may come to realize how distorted your thinking has been before.

Examples of Negative Self-Talk

Negative self-talk can eventually have an impact on your self-esteem and have a negative influence on your mental health. There are common patterns of negative thinking and self-talk:

Personalizing

If you engage in this type of negative self-talk, you blame yourself for bad things that happen without having any evidence. You beat yourself up about everything. For example, if someone is in a bad mood, you think it is about something you've done.

Catastrophizing

You always imagine the worst-case scenario. You could make a small mistake, and then you imagine that you'll lose your job and end up on the street because you're unable to pay the rent.

Filtering

You're always focusing on the negatives in your life and don't pay attention to anything positive. For example, you're having a great day, but then you go and eat somewhere, and the waitress gets your order wrong. This is all you can focus on for the rest of the day, and you don't pay any attention to the good things that happened. You're always telling yourself that only bad things happen to you.

Changing Your Negative Self-Talk

It's possible to overcome negative self-talk if you pay attention to your thinking patterns and how you can change them.

One of the first things you need to do is to become aware of the times when you're thinking negatively. Think about your thoughts, what drives them, and how they're making you feel. Keeping a journal can also make you more aware of your feelings and negative thinking.

When you become aware of negative thinking patterns, you must challenge them and establish new ways of thinking.

Your negative thoughts could be connected to irrational beliefs. You can challenge these thoughts by using positive affirmations. For example, if you find yourself thinking, "I'll never be able to do this," challenge your thoughts by saying to yourself that you're doing your best and that this is good enough. Remember that retraining your mind will take practice and time.

You can practice positive self-talk in many different ways. One of the ways is to move your attention to the positive aspects of your life. This could even be things that may seem small and insignificant to you. This is a great way to break out of a cycle of negativity.

Practicing gratitude is not only a coping skill but an overall mindset. You can practice your gratitude by keeping a journal and identifying things you're thankful for.

It could also work to step outside yourself if you're stuck in a negative cycle. Ask yourselves what your friends would say or if you would treat your best friends the same way you treat yourself.

Developing self-talk based on self-love is a powerful way to combat the cycle of negativity. Speak to yourself in the way you would speak to your loved ones and be empathetic to yourself.

At times you might have to rely on your support systems to get the negative thoughts out of your head. Talking to a friend, loved one, or even a therapist can help you determine what reality is and help you challenge your negative thinking about yourself and the world.

If your negative thoughts are too overwhelming, you may need to break and focus on something else. Visualize getting the negative thoughts away from yourself by putting them in an imaginary box. This can give you more clarity, and you can revisit these thoughts when you're in a better frame of mind. Visualization is an excellent way to manage your thinking and gain control over your thoughts.

Mindfulness and focusing on the present can also help you with negative thinking. It will give you a sense of relief and the ability to refocus.

When you find your mind wandering, you need to bring your thoughts back to the present moment. Breathing exercises and meditation can help you break free from your negative thoughts.

Cognitive Behavioral Therapy (CBT) can also help you identify negative thoughts and help you deal with how these thoughts relate to your behavior and how they influence your self-esteem. It enables you to see how you can challenge negative thinking and replace your thoughts with more positive ones.

Positive Affirmations

An affirmation is a sentence that consists of powerful words, something that's a positive statement that taps into your conscious and unconscious mind to motivate and challenge you to read your full potential in life.

We all have negative and unhealthy thoughts about ourselves and our lives at times. Positive affirmations can change how we think and act more positively and can help us reassess our beliefs about ourselves.

Affirmations have the power to help you make positive changes in your life. It can also help you get positivity back in your life and increase your self-confidence.

The best way to get affirmations to work is to repeat them daily and believe in them when you're saying them aloud. You need to repeat your affirmations at least three to five times a day for them to be more effective.

Affirmations help you focus on your strengths and make it easier for you to see yourself as worthy of understanding and kindness. To practice self-compassion, you need to accept and understand yourself.

If you are truly self-compassionate, you'll give yourself unconditional love and be fully present in your day-to-day life.

How Can You Use Affirmations to Improve Your Life?

- Take some deep breaths and smile before you start.
- Speak your affirmations slowly and as clearly as possible.
- Your body needs to absorb the positive energy of your words by saying them to yourself aloud.
- Write them down to be more specific.

Examples of Positive Affirmations

Here are some examples to get you started:

- I accept myself as I am.
- I appreciate who I am.
- I will take the time I need to heal from a bad experience and grow.
- I celebrate my uniqueness.
- I love myself.
- I accept my strengths as well as my weaknesses.
- I am proud of what I achieved.
- I deserve to have time for myself.

- I deserve love and respect.
- I am enough.
- I will be kind to myself.
- My mistakes don't define me.
- I am doing the best I can at the present time in my life.
- I will be a better friend to myself.

Interactive Element: Self-Compassion Journal

One of the best ways to get some relief from the stress in our lives, which is often self-imposed, is to keep a journal to reflect on what's really going on in your life. A self-compassion journal can help you think in new ways and could help you be kinder toward yourself. It can also help you see which expectations you need to let go of. Be honest when you're writing in this journal, and you'll be able to explore new ideas to reduce your stress levels.

After a stressful day, you may feel like falling on the couch and watching TV. However, you must sometimes confront what is stressing you out and deal with it head-on. This will take discipline, but self-reflection through journaling can help you with this process.

When you consider what is responsible for the stress in your life, you could find that it's not the external circumstances or the issue itself. Instead, you often impose unrealistic expectations, pressure, and standards on yourself.

The best way to lessen your stress could be not to tackle the issue but to have more realistic expectations of yourself. This is also where you need to have compassion for yourself.

As discussed before, self-compassion has three key elements.

- Self-kindness: We don't judge ourselves and realize that sometimes we can't avoid making mistakes. We don't get frustrated about our imperfections.

- Common humanity: We realize that other people also go through difficult times and that we're not the only ones who need to deal with difficulties that can make us feel inadequate. We can acknowledge our experiences as being part of the human condition, and we can have the same compassion for ourselves as we have for a friend or even a stranger going through hardships.

- Mindfulness: We often get caught up in our negative emotions in response to difficult situations. Mindfulness can help us distance ourselves from these thoughts and our subsequent negative emotions. It helps us notice our thoughts without judging ourselves. We can now step back and notice that we are experiencing these feelings instead of judging ourselves.

You can use these phrases, which relate to each phase, to practice self-compassion:

Self-kindness:

- I forgive myself.
- I will learn and grow from this experience.
- It is acceptable to feel like this.

Common humanity:

- All of us make mistakes.
- I am not alone.
- I am only human.

Mindfulness:

- I can look at this challenge from a different perspective.
- I'm not defined by my emotions.
- It's OK to take a step back.

Writing Prompts for Your Self-Compassion Journal

You can use one of the prompts below to get started on writing your self-compassion journal.

- Name one expectation you have of yourself that puts a lot of pressure on you. Can you remove this expectation?

- Are you currently facing stressful circumstances? What advice would you give if you had a friend or loved one in the same situation?

- Think of things you can do to take charge of what you're feeling.

- Consider a problem you faced this week and how you managed to solve it. Brainstorm other solutions that also could have worked.

- Think of a skill that you can learn to handle a stressful situation. How can you learn it?

- Think of something you can remove from your schedule to create more time for self-care.

- Think about an area in your life where you would like to be more organized. What advice would you give to a loved one or friend who wants to achieve this goal? Write down some practical action steps.

- What have you always felt scared to do? How would your friends or loved ones encourage you to overcome this fear?

- Think about how you can adjust your evening routine to get more rest at night.

- Write a letter to yourself from 10 years ago. Give advice and encouragement to your past self and help them build their self-esteem.

- How could you be gentler with yourself? Write down five ideas.

- Take a look at your to-do list. Which of the things you do isn't really necessary?

- Think of a challenge that has recently been giving you great anxiety. What advice would a friend or loved one give you when it comes to solving this problem? Also, try to see the challenge from different perspectives.

- What are you enjoying in your life at the moment? What situations are you thankful for?

Key Takeaways

- If you have compassion for someone's suffering, you "suffer with them," and you almost have the ability to feel their pain. You could feel a desire to help the person who is suffering, and you genuinely care about them.

- You're a compassionate person, which means you are understanding and kind to others when they make mistakes and fail at something. You don't judge other people for the lives they lead and the mistakes they make.

- Self-compassion means you also have the ability to be kind to yourself when you are experiencing a difficult time or when you're experiencing setbacks and failures.

- We accept the human condition of frustration and that our lives don't always go how we want them to. We understand and appreciate that other people often face the same difficulties as us.

- Most people are tougher on themselves than other people. However, this adds additional stress to life and can lead to the development of mental health problems.

- We are conditioned to see ourselves in certain ways through interaction with our childhood caretakers. Unfortunately, if you had hypercritical caretakers, you could develop an extremely critical inner voice.

- Many people judge themselves as being unworthy, as they base their values on the childhood expectations placed on them, such as expectations of how they have to perform. If they're not performing up to their own harsh expectations, that can develop unhealthy self-esteem.

- Our self-critical perceptions of whether we can live up to our values will impact our self-worth.

- Your behavior will be influenced by the perception you have of yourself.

- Self-kindness is about still being kind to yourself when you make mistakes and not being overly critical of yourself when you're in pain.

- A shared/common humanity means we need to see our individual experiences as being embedded in the broader human experience. It's not good for your mental health to view yourself as being separate or isolated from others and see yourself as the only one who is suffering at that time.

- Your shortcomings are part of the human condition, and you should see them as such. You need to see your difficulties as being part of life that other people go through as well. Everyone feels inadequate and inefficient at times.

- Mindfulness encourages self-compassion, as it will decrease your tendency to judge yourself. Mindfulness can help you keep your perspective if you fail at things that are important to you. It will also help you better adapt to your emotions when you're feeling sad or negative.

- Another way to practice self-compassion is to develop a growth mindset. People who cultivate a growth mindset often find themselves not only better able to deal with day-to-day challenges but also unexpected hardships that may come along.

- When you find yourself becoming self-critical, treat yourself with kindness and speak to yourself as you would speak to your best friend. If you find you're saying things to yourself that you won't say to other people, stop doing so.

- Negative self-talk can make us feel angry and depressed. This could cause us to start acting in self-destructive ways.

- Positive self-talk will help you replace your negative thinking with positive ones.

- You can overcome negative thinking by paying attention to your thinking patterns and how you can change them.

- Practicing gratitude is an overall mindset. You can practice your gratitude by keeping a journal and identifying things you're thankful for. At the end of every day, think of people and things you have in your life that you are grateful for.

- Developing self-talk based on self-love is a powerful way to combat the cycle of negativity. Always treat yourself with empathy.

- We all have negative and unhealthy thoughts about ourselves and our lives at times. Positive affirmations can help us reassess our beliefs and encourage us to act in more positive ways.

- You need to repeat your positive affirmations a few times a day and believe what you're saying.

- Affirmations help you focus on your strengths and make it easier to see yourself as someone worthy of love and understanding.

- When you consider what is really responsible for the stress in your life, you could discover that it is the unrealistic expectations, pressure, and standards that you impose on yourself that are the main problem. It's usually not an external stressor.

Chapter 8:

Build Connections

Eating healthy and getting enough exercise are often touted as the secrets to a long life. However, a rich and productive life is more likely to guarantee longevity. Part of such a lifestyle is meaningful connections to others, be it our loved ones, friends, or colleagues at work.

We are social beings who seek to also enrich our lives through the connections we form with the people we want in our lives. Our social connections can also play an important role in forming our identities.

Why Do We Need to Connect?

As human beings, we are social creatures who have the need to connect with each other. When you look back on history, you'll see that people have always existed, traveled, and hunted in groups. Social groups provide most people with a big part of their identities and teach them the skills they need to succeed in a complex environment.

For many of us, feeling socially connected in a world that is becoming increasingly isolated is more important than ever.

Social connections can have the following positive effects:

- They can help you improve the quality of your life. Social connections can keep you healthy. It doesn't mean always being physically present with people, but more that you feel understood and connected to others.

- Connection can also boost your mental health. Having friends can boost your mental health by giving you an increased sense of belonging, confidence, and purpose, as well as increasing your general levels of happiness, reducing your stress levels, and improving your self-worth. People who don't have sufficient social support are more likely to suffer from mental health problems like anxiety and depression.

- Forming strong bonds with other people also decreases suicide risk. Strong relationships can play a vital role in protecting people against suicidal thoughts and behaviors.

If you're unsure how to begin forming social connections, start by looking inward. Consider what your interests are and which hobbies you enjoy. What kind of people do you enjoy being around? Become active in your community, spend some time volunteering or join clubs and social organizations. If you meet someone you want to spend time with, create opportunities to spend time together.

You need to keep in mind that social connections that are going to impact your overall health are going to need time and effort. If you want to form healthy relationships with others, you need to open up, listen actively and share what you're going through. It can feel scary to establish a bond with others, but it's crucial to put yourself out there and form relationships that can change the course of your life.

Random Acts of Kindness

Random acts of kindness are when you do something good for someone else without expecting anything in return.

We've usually learned what kindness is through years of experience, and what the intention behind someone's kindness could be.

People are more likely to be kind to those who they have a closer relationship with.

How Can Kindness Impact Our Well-Being?

If we're recipients of an act of kindness, it could make us feel more loved. Whether you're the recipient or giver of kindness, you can experience the benefits of an increase in oxytocin. Oxytocin is referred to as the "love hormone" and can help lower our blood pressure, improve our heart health, and increase our optimism and self-esteem.

Being kind can also make us feel less depressed and increase our feelings of self-worth. Kindness can push your body to produce more of the "feel-good" chemical serotonin, which can improve healing and also help you calm your feelings.

Kindness can also decrease physical pain by generating more of the brain's natural painkillers, namely endorphins. Kind people usually have less cortisol (stress hormone) in their bodies, and they also tend to age more slowly than the rest of the population. Being kind can also reduce your blood pressure, and oxytocin is also known as the "cardioprotective" hormone. This hormone can protect your heart by lowering your blood pressure.

We're also creating new connections in our brains by thinking compassionate thoughts. Our emotions can form the structures of our brains by forming connections between the cells. These connections can become very extensive over time.

We keep on learning new things throughout our lives as we grow as people and change our habits, which will also lead to new connections being formed in our brains.

Some Ideas for Random Acts of Kindness

There are many small ways that you can be kind to all the people in your life, as well as strangers around you. Let's take a look at some of them:

- Give compliments to random people that you interact with throughout the day.

- Smile and greet strangers you walk past during the day.

- Give up your seat on public transport for someone who needs it.

- When you're waiting for a takeaway coffee, offer to pay for the person standing behind you.

- Send an email to your coworkers to tell them that you appreciate your help.

The Stress-Reducing Conversations

The way you communicate can help you build an emotional connection with people. If you're capable of communicating well, you can open up to people without the fear of being judged. Dialogues such as asking someone how their day was, can reaffirm trust between people, but it's not entirely enough.

Having a stress-reducing conversation can help you manage your daily stress so that outside stressors won't spill into your relationship.

Couples who find themselves in stressful situations often find stress from other areas in their lives, such as problems at work, spilling over into their relationship and leading to conflict.

Failure to handle this stress can ultimately harm intimate relationships. However, if you're in a relationship and talk about the stress about your partner, you're more likely to keep your relationship strong.

When you talk about your stress, it is also vital that the timing is suitable for all parties involved, as while some people want to vent immediately, others may wish to decompress before they're ready. You'll need to agree on what works for you.

The main rule of the stress-reducing relationship is that you should only talk about the stress that falls outside your relationship. Don't discuss areas of conflict between you. This is also not the right time to tell your partner to fix their problems. Now is the time that you should be supporting each other emotionally.

While these conversations aren't about your relationship, stress-reducing conversations have the ability to improve relationships. These conversations will allow you to connect on an intimate level as the emotional attraction will normally grow when you feel someone is listening to you, respects your perspectives, and also cares genuinely about you.

How to Have a Stress-Reducing Conversation

There are easy ways to have a stress-reducing conversation. For your conversation to work, you need to employ the technique of "active listening."

The goal is to listen to the speaker with empathy and without judgment. There are seven rules for having this type of discussion:

1. Take turns when voicing your concerns. Allow your partner to state their complaints without interrupting them.

2. Listen to your partner, and don't give them unsolicited advice. You must understand their perspective before you can really discuss anything.

3. Stay focused on your partner during the conversation. Show genuine interest in what you're saying, and don't let your mind and eyes wander.

4. Communicate to your partner that you empathize with what they're saying. Be supportive of your partner when they give you their perspective, even if you think it's unreasonable. Your relationship should be more important to you than your opinion on the topic.

5. Make your partner understand that you're in this together. You need to have a united front against whatever strives to divide you.

6. Express affection during your conversation with your partner. This could be verbal but physical as well, such as giving them a hug.

7. Also, tell your partner that their feelings make sense to you.

The Importance of Physical Connection

In today's busy world, relationships have often become an act of convenience. However, physical intimacy should also be about the connection between people.

When the initial attraction between a couple fades, you get the true testing phase of the relationship. If you can pass this test and the relationship lasts beyond the initial connection, you can know it will be for the long term.

The Importance of Touch

If you don't get as much physical touch as you used to, or even no touch at all, you can experience touch starvation. This could also happen when you want contact but can't seem to interact with others for some reason.

Touch is an important way how we as humans interact with each other. We bond through physical touch, for example, by hugging people and shaking hands.

Skin is our largest organ and can send good and bad touch sensations to our brains. If you experience pleasant touch, like a hug or kiss, your brain will release the hormone oxytocin. This will make you feel good and help you form strong emotional and social bonds.

Human touch can also help you regulate your sleeping cycle and digestion, help you build your immune system, and fight infections.

You can become stressed, anxious, and stressed when you suffer from touch starvation. Your body will make a hormone called cortisol in response to stress. This will increase your heart rate and muscle tension, and your blood pressure and breathing rate will go up. Your immune and digestive systems will also be negatively affected.

If you experience starvation in the long term, it could even lead to posttraumatic stress disorder (PTSD).

You can fight touch starvation, even when you can't interact in person with them.

Video chat can let you visually interact with other people, and this can help you ease your symptoms.

Online yoga and workout classes can help you interact in a friendly environment, which might make you feel less lonely.

Singing and dancing can boost your oxycontin levels when you can't physically interact with people.

Even playing with your pets can help you relax and ease your touch starvation symptoms. Dog owners' oxytocin levels also peak when they're caressing their pets.

Physical Affection in Relationships

There are normally different types of physical affection in a relationship, for example, hugging, cuddling, caressing, backrubs, holding hands, and kissing on the lips and face.

Physical affection doesn't have to be limited to love relationships. For example, if one of your friends pats you on the back, it can also be seen as a physical connection that could boost your morale.

Connection With Animals

Pets can be joyful, loyal companions, especially when you may not have that many supportive people in your life. Pets could decrease your stress levels, improve your heart health, and could even help children improve their social and emotional skills.

So, what health benefits can pets bring you? Interacting with your pets can decrease your cortisol levels and lower your blood pressure. Animals can boost your mood by reducing your loneliness and can increase your feelings of social support.

You can also benefit from having a dog if you want to increase your physical activity. When you walk your dog several times a day, you'll increase your physical activity. If you want to reduce your stress levels, an activity like watching your pet fish swim can make you feel calmer. Your cat sitting, purring beside you, can also provide you some comfort after a long day at work.

Pets can also help you meet new people and start and maintain friendships. Dog owners often stop and talk to each other when walking their pets, while they are on hikes, or in the dog park.

Having a pet can also add structure and routine to your days. Most pets have a regular exercise and feeding schedule. A consistent routine will keep your pet calm and balanced and will also do the same for you.

You will have to figure out what pet will work best for you.

Animals can also help people who are going through physical or mental health struggles. Therapy dogs are sometimes brought into hospitals or nursing homes to help patients reduce their stress and anxiety levels.

Dogs can also understand some of the words we use, and they can also understand our body language, tone of voice, and our gestures. A dog will also try to understand your emotional state, thoughts, and feelings. This will help them figure out when they'll get their next treat or walk.

One of the reasons why a pet is beneficial for your health and can help lower your cholesterol and blood pressure levels is because they fulfill the human need for touch. People with pets are also less likely to develop depression.

Benefits for Older Adults

Having a pet can also help you age in a healthier way if you're older. Pets can help you find renewed meaning in life.

Retired people often have a lot of time on their hands if they've retired or their children have moved away. Pets can add more meaning to their lives.

Having a dog can also help you stay connected, as maintaining social connections can be challenging as you get older.

Pets can also boost your playfulness and vitality and encourage you to get exercise.

Spirituality

You can also find stress relief through spirituality. This does not necessarily involve religion or a specific belief system. Spirituality arises from your connection with yourself and others, the development of your personal values, and your search for meaning in life.

Spirituality is different for everyone. While you might find yours in nature, art, or music, others will discover theirs as part of religious observance, prayer, or meditation.

Finding your spirituality can have the following benefits for your mental health:

- It can help you find a sense of purpose. Your spirituality may help you uncover what is most meaningful in your life. If you clarify what's important to you, you can focus less on unimportant things and decrease the stress in your life.

- Spirituality helps you connect to the world and find your purpose. This will make you feel less alone, even when you're lonely, and you can gain a sense of inner peace.

- Spirituality helps you realize and appreciate that you aren't responsible for everything that happens and goes wrong in life.

People who are spiritual are normally also better able to cope with stress.

How Can You Discover Your Spirituality

It could take you some time to discover your spirituality. You can ask yourself questions like:

- What do you value in your life?

- What are you proud of achieving?

- What brings you joy?

- What type of people make you feel a sense of community?

The answers to these types of questions can help you find the most important experiences in your life. When you have this information, you can focus on searching for your spirituality, and you can also focus on relationships and activities that have helped define you as a person and that inspire your personal growth.

A main element of spirituality involves getting in touch with your inner self. You can do this in the following ways:

- Prayer, mindfulness, meditation, and relaxation techniques can help you focus your thoughts and find peace of mind.

- Find an advisor or friend who can help you discover what is important in your life. Other people may have insights that you haven't discovered yet.

- Write your thoughts in a journal to record your progress and express your feelings.

- Read inspirational essays and stories to become used to different views and philosophies of life.

- Talk to other people whose spiritual lives you admire. Ask them questions and discover more about how they found their ways to more fulfilling spiritual lives.

- Your spirituality can also be nurtured through your relationships with others. It's very important to foster good relationships with the people you care about. Make your friends and family a priority and try to see the good in people and yourself.

- Do your best to see others as they are without judging them. It's also a great idea to contribute to your community through volunteering.

- Your life and the lives of those around you can be enhanced by staying connected to your inner spirit. Staying in contact with your spirituality may change through your life experiences, but this will always form the basis of your well-being and help you cope with stress throughout your life.

Why You Should Sometimes Put Yourself First

We often spend a lot of time feeling stressed and running around while looking after everyone else's needs. The healthiest thing to do in these types of situations is often to step away and think about how we can take care of ourselves.

This may seem obvious to many people, but many of us don't really like the idea of putting ourselves first. We were raised (especially women) and conditioned to think we should always put others before ourselves and ignore our needs and wants. If we care for ourselves, we fear we can be seen as arrogant or self-centered.

So, why are so many of us so reluctant to care for ourselves?

As stated before, we think self-care is selfish. However, it's actually the opposite of this, as it makes us stronger and better able to care for our loved ones. Do you ever wonder why flight attendants advise you to put your own oxygen mask on first before helping anybody else in case of emergency? This is because we can't really help anyone if our own energy is depleted. Self-care can help us overcome stress, as it builds our resilience which helps us better cope with challenges. Support others where you can but pay attention to yourself first.

We often don't engage in self-care because we're too busy helping everyone else. However, you can't really save other people and decide what is good for them. This is something they can only do for themselves. You're just denying them the opportunity to face their own challenges and grow from the experience. By rescuing people through what we believe is love, we're just enabling someone to stay helpless while we are suffering from stress. Support people, but don't take it on yourself to save someone and try to steer their lives in a direction you think they should go.

We're also used to relationships that are based on neediness and not real love. We like the idea of love because we've watched many Hollywood films that portray love as dramatic and exciting and that you need to be with someone 24/7. We end up giving too much in our love relationships as we believe we should die for someone else and other dramatic things, and we forget that we are unique, too, and end up losing ourselves in the process of loving someone else. It's much healthier to focus on ourselves than spend every waking hour thinking about someone else. This way, we can give to others from a place of wholeness without expecting anything in return or resenting other people. If we're more independent and less needy of affection and attention, we're better able to connect with other people.

We teach people how to treat us through our actions and the attitude we have toward ourselves. If you send out signals that you're willing to sacrifice yourself to save others, you'll just attract the type of people who want to be rescued, and your relationship will end up being all about them. Remember that your self-care is your responsibility. Many people will treat you like a doormat if you allow them to do so.

We could expect others to take care of us, even though we think we don't, and we end up resentful if the other person can't give back in equal measure.

We could also think others are worth more than us, and we aren't confident in our love for ourselves. If we treat ourselves as if we're worthy, this is what we'll attract back into our lives.

Interactive Element: Self-Care List

Make yourself a list of self-care activities you enjoy. You could use some of the following suggestions:

- Eat three healthy meals a day and avoid eating too many sugary snacks.
- Do some exercise every day.
- Spend time in the sun outside every day.
- Try to do creative activities you enjoy when you have time.
- Spend time with positive people.
- Set healthy boundaries and say no to people when you need to.
- Treat myself with kindness and be my own best friend.
- Pause before you do something and consider if this is something you really want to do.

You can continue adding your own items to the list.

Key Takeaways

- Humans are social beings, and we enrich our lives through our connections with others.

- In today's world, which is becoming increasingly isolated, it's more important than ever to have some type of social connection.

- Social connections are also very important for your mental health. Having friends can boost your mental health by giving you an increased sense of belonging, confidence, and purpose in life. If you have a few friends, your general level of happiness will be higher, your stress levels lower, and you'll have higher self-esteem.

- If you want to boost your chances of forming social connections, think about your hobbies and interests. What do you enjoy doing? Try to join groups of people with the same interests, for example, book clubs or hiking clubs. You could even join online groups.

- It will help you to form healthy relationships with others if you can open up, listen actively, and share with others what you're experiencing.

- When you give or receive kindness, you can experience an increase in oxytocin. Oxytocin is referred to as the "love hormone" and can help lower your blood pressure. It could also improve your heart health and increase your optimism and self-esteem.

- Being kind can even increase your feelings of self-worth and make you feel less depressed. Kindness can push your body to produce more serotonin, which can make you feel better and heal faster.

- Couples may find that stress from other areas in their lives, such as problems at work, spilling over into their romantic relationship and leading to conflict.

- When you're having a stress-reducing conversation, you need to be able to listen with empathy and without judging the speaker. For your conversation to work, you need to employ the technique of "active listening."

- Physical intimacy is about the connection between people. It is essential for our health that we get a certain amount of physical contact on a regular basis. If you don't get as much physical touch as you used to, or even no touch at all, you can experience touch starvation.

- Humans often interact through touch. We bond through physical touch, for example, by hugging people and shaking hands.

- Skin is our largest organ and can send good and bad touch sensations to our brains. If you experience pleasant touch, like a hug or kiss, your brain will release the hormone oxytocin.

- Human touch can have an array of benefits for your health. Not only can it help you regulate your sleeping cycle and digestion, but it can also assist you with building your immune system and fighting infections.

- People who suffer from touch starvation tend to become stressed and anxious. Their bodies will make a hormone called cortisol in response to stress. This will increase their heart rates, cause muscle tension, and increase their blood pressure and breathing. Their immune and digestive system will also be negatively affected.

- Physical affection doesn't have to be limited to love relationships. For example, any type of physical touch can boost your morale.

- Pets can be joyful and loyal companions. They're good for your mental health, especially at times when you maybe don't have that many supportive people in your life. Touching your pets can also make up for the lack of human touch.

- Interacting with your pets can decrease your cortisol levels and lower your blood pressure. Your pets can also boost your mood by reducing your loneliness and can increase your feelings of social support.

- Animals can also help people who are going through physical or mental health struggles. Therapy dogs are sometimes brought into hospitals or nursing homes to help patients and reduce their stress and anxiety levels.

- Dogs can understand some of the words we use, and they can also understand our body language, tone of voice, and our gestures. Pets, such as dogs, can also try to understand your emotional state and what you're thinking and feeling. This will help them figure out when they can get their next treat or walk.

- Spirituality arises from your connection with yourself and others, the development of your personal values, and your search for meaning in life. It doesn't have to include religion. However, many people do find their spirituality in religion.

- Your spirituality can help you uncover what is most meaningful in your life. If you clarify what's important to you, it will decrease your stress levels, as you will focus less on things that are unimportant to you.

- Spirituality helps you connect to the world and find your purpose. This will make you feel less alone, even when you're lonely, and you can gain a sense of inner peace.

- Getting in touch with yourself is a main element of spirituality.

- You can also nurture your spirituality through your interaction with others. It's vital to foster good relationships with the people you care about.

- We often spend a lot of time feeling stressed and running around while looking after the needs of everyone else. It's often healthier to step away, especially when you're not feeling that great yourself, to also make time to take care of yourself.

- Many people don't like the idea of putting themselves first. We were raised (especially women) and conditioned to think that we should always put others, such as family members and children, before ourselves and ignore our own needs and wants. We fear we will be regarded as arrogant and selfish if we take the time to care for ourselves.

Conclusion

Reading this book is your first step to recovery from burnout. You now have the confidence and knowledge to make lasting changes to your life. You would have learned that self-care is one of the most important practical tools to help you prevent burnout and recover from it.

To prevent long-term burnout, you need to start seeing yourself as valuable and that you're worthwhile enough to care for yourself. While this book can provide you with the tools, it's up to you to take the necessary steps to look after yourself. It could potentially be a long journey, but you've already taken the first steps to becoming a healthier version of yourself and leading a more meaningful life.

When you're emotionally, physically, and mentally exhausted, burnout can be worrying because it can make you more vulnerable to illness, causing long-term changes to your body. This can lead to serious chronic conditions like high blood pressure and diabetes.

In the workplace, many businesses are taking burnout more seriously, and it is even regarded as a crisis since so many employees are experiencing it. As discussed in the introduction, since the advent of the Covid-19 pandemic and the work-from-home situation, companies and employees have been experiencing new ways of working, which has brought new challenges along with it.

Unfortunately, it's usually the high performers that end up with burnout, as they could end up being burdened with the bulk of the work and responsibilities, especially if a workplace doesn't have a well-functioning management process in place.

A Constant State of Stress: Completing Your Stress Cycle

Nowadays, it's not unusual for many of us to constantly feel stressed. Part of the reason we end up feeling so bad is that we never complete our stress cycles. As we explained in more detail earlier in the book, we only really complete a stress cycle once our bodies accept that we are safe again, after we go through a process of facing danger.

When it comes to stress and our health, completing the stress cycle is one of the most important things we can do for our mental health. If we don't confront our stress, the danger is that our bodies will stay in a constant hyper-alert stage, with elevated blood pressure, which could lead to a higher chance that we could develop heart disease and digestion issues.

It's a good idea to actively work toward completing your stress cycle. You can do this by getting at least two to three hours of physical activity during the week. This can include anything from walking to dancing or whatever can get you off the couch, out of your house, and moving. Don't worry if you can't get out of your house; it's perfectly fine moving around inside your house as well. Put the radio on and dance to the music, or if you are one of those people who have a piece of exercise equipment, such as a cycle or treadmill, good for you! Jump on it and get going.

Creativity can also help you a great deal with completing your stress cycle. Make sure you choose something you really enjoy doing, whether it's creative writing, cooking creative meals, or baking delicious cakes.

When it comes to completing the stress cycle, one of the most important things you can do is to make sure that you get enough sleep. A good night's sleep will boost your recovery from stressful events.

Stress will always be a part of our lives, and we won't be able to avoid it. However, we can manage our reactions to stress.

Imagination and Creativity Can Give You a Better Life

If you can imagine yourself in a better position, you'll never be a victim of your circumstances. You'll find ways to get ahead, even if you're facing obstacles that seem impossible to overcome.

Remember that one of the first steps to a happier future is to imagine it. People with an optimistic outlook are able to look past their present challenges and see themselves living happier and more productive lives in the future.

You almost want to be like a child and have the ability to change your life into something magical by using your imagination. Imagination can help you think outside the box when it comes to your career and also your personal life.

Getting involved in creative activities and new art forms can get your creative juices flowing. Even if you think you don't have an artistic bone in your body, practicing new art skills can unleash your creativity and ultimately help you think differently about your life.

Expressing Your Emotions

Creative expression can be an excellent outlet for overwhelming thoughts and feelings. It's better for your mental health to express your feelings honestly, as you acknowledge and recognize what you're feeling instead of denying it.

As we've established, artistic activities can be beneficial in a therapeutic way. They can free your unconscious mind and are considered a healthy form of escapism. Creativity can also help us externalize our thought processes and help us observe our feelings from a distance, which will help us not to act impulsively about them.

You'll find inner healing if you let your emotions flow and create something that connects you to other people or helps you touch their hearts.

Humor could also help you get through some tough situations. Cracking jokes can help you get through the daily stresses and will also make it easier for you to deal with whatever life throws at you. So, enjoy watching your favorite comedy shows on television.

149

The Physical Aspects of Burnout

If you don't get enough sleep or exercise, or your diet is not up to scratch, this situation can exacerbate your burnout. Sleep helps you recharge, and if you don't sleep enough, your life can be affected in so many negative ways. For example, you could struggle to concentrate and formulate your thoughts, and your memory will also be affected.

Taking a Break and Pausing

We all need to take breaks from the noise and the never-ending frantic activity to re-energize ourselves. Our nervous systems can only regain a sense of balance when we give ourselves time to relax and to be quiet.

Sometimes we need to find our inner peace and silence before we can discover what is bothering us and start our recovery from burnout. Pausing can help us refocus our energy and make us better able to handle challenging moments. For example, it's easier to solve your problems if your brain is less busy with all kinds of anxious thoughts. Taking a pause can give our nervous system the opportunity to regain its balance and help us become more resilient to stress. You'll also be able to shift your perspective to what is truly important to you.

Overall, pausing can help you deal better with the stress you face in your life.

All of us have negative thoughts about ourselves and our lives at times. However, to get ahead and make changes in life, we need to be able to reassess our beliefs about ourselves, and positive affirmations can help us do this.

The best way to get your positive affirmations to work is to repeat them a few times a day and to believe in saying them when you say them aloud to yourself. They can help you see yourself as a worthy human being who deserves understanding and kindness.

Taking Care of Yourself

Finally, if you're burned out or on the verge of burning out, it means you've used more energy than your body can expend. You may feel that you have a lot to prove to everyone around you, but it's also important to prioritize your mental health above your goals. When you've already experienced the harmful effects of overworking, you don't want it to become worse. It's important that you learn to live mindfully and pace yourself by not taking on too much.

If you live with self-awareness and self-control, you'll be able to achieve so much more in life.

Personal Note From the Author

I want to wish you the best of luck on your journey to self-discovery and your recovery from burnout. I've enjoyed sharing my knowledge with you, and I trust that I have given you the foundation to overcome burnout.

It could be a lengthy journey, depending on where you find yourself in your life, but I'm proud of you for taking the first steps to putting yourself first. Remember, we can't care for others if we don't care for ourselves first. Never feel guilty about caring for yourself, as this is the first step to leading a better and more fulfilling life.

I look forward to your feedback and hearing how the book has helped you. If so, I would really appreciate it if you would leave your reviews on Amazon.

Scan the QR Code below to leave
a review on Amazon!

References

Apollo Technical. (May 16, 2022). *Startling remote work burnout statistics (2021) | Apollo Technical.* https://www.apollotechnical.com/remote-work-burnout-statistics/

Asp, K. (2020, January 22). *Quantity of sleep Vs quality of sleep: Why this is Important?* Www.aastweb.org. https://www.aastweb.org/blog/quantity-of-sleep-vs-quality-of-sleep-why-this-is-important

Bala, S. (2022, July 5). *These major economies are headed into recession in the next 12 months, Nomura says.* CNBC. https://www.cnbc.com/2022/07/05/us-uk-europe-japan-will-be-in-recession-over-next-12-months-nomura-.html

Beheshti, N. (2021, April 15). *The pandemic has created a new kind of burnout, which makes well-being more critical than ever.* Forbes. https://www.forbes.com/sites/nazbeheshti/2021/04/15/the-pandemic-has-created-a-new-kind-of-burnout-which-makes-well-being-more-critical-than-ever/?sh=4b1ca4ab2f01

Benisek, A. (2021, April 19). *Touch starvation: What to know.* WebMD. https://www.webmd.com/balance/touch-starvation

Bisht, P. (2021, Mar 16). *Why imagination is important and how to use it?* https://www.linkedin.com/pulse/why-imagination-important-how-use-pawan-bishtBreaus, M. (September 9, 2022). *Chronotype quiz.* The Sleep Doctor. https://thepowerofwhenquiz.com

Brennan, D. (2020, December 3). *Burnout: symptoms and signs.* WebMD. https://www.webmd.com/mental-health/burnout-symptoms-signs

Burgess, L. (2017, October 17) *Benefits of crying: Why do we cry, and when to seek support.* Www.medicalnewstoday.com. https://www.medicalnewstoday.com/articles/319631

Calming Grace. (September 22, 2020). 30 Self-Compassion Journal Prompts for Stress Relief. Calming Grace. https://www.calminggrace.com/self-compassion-journal-prompts/

Dietrich, M. (Mar 11, 2015). *Time for a pleasure pause?* Madelinedietrich.com. https://madelinedietrich.com/blog/single/time_for_a_pleasure_pause

Dixon, E. (June 23, 2020) *Harnessing The power of imagination.* Psychology Today. https://www.psychologytoday.com/us/blog/the-flourishing-family/202006/harnessing-the-power-imagination

Elkin, A. (March 26, 2016). *How to use your imagination to de-stress.* Dummies.com https://www.dummies.com/article/body-mind-spirit/emotional-health-psychology/emotional-health/stress/how-to-use-your-imagination-to-de-stress-164564/

Ellie Lisitsa. (June 22, 2013). *How to have a stress-reducing conversation.* The Gottman Institute.

https://www.gottman.com/blog/how-to-stress-reducing-conversation/

Ellis, R. (January 10, 2019). *Surprising reasons to get more sleep.* WebMD. https://www.webmd.com/sleep-disorders/benefits-sleep-more

Embrace Sexual Wellness. (December 17, 2020). *Stress cycles: what they are and how to break them.* https://www.embracesexualwellness.com/esw-blog/stresscycles

Feminist Survival Project 2020. (2020, September 6) *Episode 47: Pause for pleasure.* https://www.feministsurvivalproject.com/episodes/episode-47-pause-for-pleasure

Gungor, Michael. (2012). *The Crowd, The Critic, and The Muse: A Book for Creators.* Woodsley Press.

Health, I. (November 5, 2021). *What are the 5 stages of burnout?* Integrisok.com. https://integrisok.com/resources/on-your-health/2021/november/what-are-the-5-stages-of-burnout

Matthews, D. (2019, September 25). *Creative self-expression for health, coping, and resilience.* Psychology Today. https://www.psychologytoday.com/us/blog/going-beyond-intelligence/201909/creative-self-expression-health-coping-and-resilience

Mayo Clinic Staff. (August 18, 2020). *Exercise and stress: Get moving to manage stress.* Mayo Clinic. https://www.mayoclinic.org/healthy-lifestyle/stress-management/in-depth/exercise-and-stress/art-20044469

MedlinePlus. (August 30, 2017). *Benefits of exercise*. Medlineplus.gov; National Library of Medicine. https://medlineplus.gov/benefitsofexercise.html

Mezick, E. (n.d.). *Encyclopedia of behavioral medicine*, 1805–1806. Sleep Continuity. https://doi.org/10.1007/978-1-4419-1005-9_843

Mindhelp. (n.d.). *Online burnout test - mind help (Self-Assessment)*. https://mind.help/assessments/burnout-test/

Mindtool.com. (n.d.). *Burnout self-test: – Are you at risk?* Mindtools.com. https://www.mindtools.com/pages/article/newTCS_08.htm

MindWise Innovations. (July 24, 2017). *The importance of social connection*. MindWise. https://www.mindwise.org/blog/uncategorized/the-importance-of-social-connection/

Moore, C. (June 2, 2019). *How to practice self-compassion: 8 techniques and tips*. PositivePsychology.com. https://positivepsychology.com/how-to-practice-self-compassion/

Neff, K. (n.d.). *Definition and three elements of self-compassion*. Self-Compassion. https://self-compassion.org/the-three-elements-of-self-compassion-2/

Nyce, C. M. (2022, September 13). *The Cure for Burnout Is Not Self-Care*. The Atlantic. https://www.theatlantic.com/ideas/archive/2022/09/what-is-quiet-quitting-burnout-at-work/671413/

Ohlin, B. (October 9, 2016). *5 Steps to develop self-compassion & overcome your inner critic.* PositivePsychology.com. https://positivepsychology.com/self-compassion-5-steps/

Pacheco, D. (January 8, 2021). *Chronotypes: definition, types, & effect on sleep.* Sleep Foundation. https://www.sleepfoundation.org/how-sleep-works/chronotypes

Psych Central. (June 22, 2022). *How to complete the stress response cycle.* Psych Central. https://psychcentral.com/stress/the-stress-response-cycle#_noHeaderPrefixedContent

Psych Central. (June 23, 2022). *Mindful Moment: The healing potential of creative self-expression.* https://psychcentral.com/health/mindful-moment-creative-self-expression

Psych Central. (November 2, 2021). *How stress affects you physically.* Psych Central. https://psychcentral.com/stress/the-physical-effects-of-long-term-stress#physical-effects

Psych Central. (September 12, 2021). *Challenging negative thoughts: helpful tips.* Psych Central. https://psychcentral.com/lib/challenging-negative-self-talk

Psychology Tools. (n.d.) *Fight or flight response.* https://www.psychologytools.com/resource/fight-or-flight-response/

Ritchie, J. (July 21, 2016). *Why we put ourselves last & why self-care should be a priority.* Tiny Buddha.

https://tinybuddha.com/blog/why-put-ourselves-last-why-self-care-priority/

Robinson, L., Lundgren, K., & Segal, R. (February 13, 2019). *Mood-boosting power of dogs*. HelpGuide.org. https://www.helpguide.org/articles/mental-health/mood-boosting-power-of-dogs.htm

Rodquist-Kodet, A. (November 17, 2020) *Completing our body's stress response cycle | UK Human Resources*. (n.d.). https://www.uky.edu/hr/thrive/11-17-2020/completing-our-bodys-stress-response-cycle

Rotar, S. (February 5, 2022) *45 Self-compassion affirmations to practice when feeling Low* - Mental Style Project. https://mentalstyleproject.com/45-self-compassion-affirmations/

Samson, P. (September 3, 2020). *What the F*** is a mindful pause?* Mr Feelgood. https://mrfeelgood.com/articles/wtf-is-a-mindful-pause

Sayer, A. (December 27, 2021). *Here are the best workouts for beginners to get you moving*. The Manual. https://www.themanual.com/fitness/best-workouts-for-beginners/

Scott, J. (n.d.). *Self expression art, humor and music*. https://drjimscott.weebly.com/self-expression-art-humor-and-music.html

Smith, M., Segal, J., & Robinson, L. (December 27, 2018). *Burnout prevention and treatment*. HelpGuide.org. https://www.helpguide.org/articles/stress/burnout-prevention-and-recovery.htm

Sparks, D. (April 3, 2019). *Mayo Mindfulness: Connecting spirituality and stress relief.* Mayo Clinic News Network. https://newsnetwork.mayoclinic.org/discussion/mayo-mindfulness-connecting-spirituality-and-stress-relief/

Stoerkel, E. (July 4, 2019). *Can random acts of kindness increase wellbeing?* PositivePsychology.com. https://positivepsychology.com/random-acts-kindness/

Sukel, K. (February 27, 2019) *Harnessing imagination to calm fears.* Dana Foundation. https://www.dana.org/article/harnessing-imagination-to-calm-fears/

Tanti, R (July 2, 2021). *The importance of affirmations.* https://www.ymcansw.org.au/news-and-media/the-y-at-home/the-importance-of-affirmations/

Todorov, G. (December 29, 2021). *Important burnout statistics, trends and facts 2022 - Learn Digital Marketing.* Thrivemyway.com. https://thrivemyway.com/burnout-stats/

Wellteq. (2022, June 20). *What's the difference between fatigue, burnout and exhaustion?* https://wellteq.co/insights/mental-health/fatigue-burnout-and-exhaustion-whats-the-difference/

Youth Empowerment. (November 6, 2021). *Challenging negative self-talk.* https://youthempowerment.com/challenging-negative-self-talk/